# How to Be a Christian Without Being PEЯFECT

# Fritz Ridenour

**AUTHOR OF THE BEST-SELLING
"HOW TO BE A CHRISTIAN WITHOUT BEING RELIGIOUS"**

# How to Be a Christian Without Being PEЯFECT

*A Life-Related Study of I John*

## Regal Books

A Division of GL Publications
Ventura, California, U.S.A.

Rights for publishing this book in other languages are contracted by Gospel Literature International (GLINT) foundation. GLINT also provides technical help for the adaptation, translation, and publishing of Bible study resources and books in scores of languages worldwide. For further information, contact GLINT, Post Office Box 6688, Ventura, California 93006, U.S.A., or the publisher.

Except where otherwise indicated, Scripture quotations in this book are from:
*NIV—Holy Bible: The New International Version.* Copyright © 1978 by the International Bible Society. Used by permission of Zondervan Bible Publishers. Also quoted are:
*KJV—Authorized King James Version.*
*TLB—*From *The Living Bible,* Copyright © 1971 by Tyndale House Publishers, Wheaton, Illinois. Used by permission.
*NASB—New American Standard Bible.* © The Lockman Foundation 1960, 1962, 1963, 1968, 1971, 1972, 1973, 1975. Used by permission.
*NEB—*From *The New English Bible.* © The Delegates of the Oxford University Press and The Syndics of the Cambridge University Press, 1961, 1970. Reprinted by permission.
*AMP—Amplified Bible, The.* Copyright © 1962, 1964 by Zondervan Publishing House. Used by permission.
*Phillips—The New Testament in Modern English,* Revised Edition, J.B. Phillips, Translator. © J.B. Phillips 1958, 1960, 1972. Used by permission of Macmillan Publishing Co., Inc.

Published by Regal Books
A Division of GL Publications
Ventura, California 93006
Printed in U.S.A.

**Library of Congress Cataloging in Publication Data**

Ridenour, Fritz
   How to be a Christian without being perfect.

   1. Bible. N.T. Epistles of John, 1st—Criticism, interpretation, etc. 2. Christian life—1960—   . I. Title.
BS2805.2.R53       1986        227'.9407       86-6479
    ISBN 0-8307-1106-6         ISBN 0-8307-1167-8
     (Trade Edition)           (Hardcover Edition)

**1 2 3 4 5 6 7 8 9 10 / 91 90 89 88 87 86**

# Dedication

To the Adult Sunday School Classes
of
Trinity Bible Fellowship
Fullerton, California
and
Evangelical Free Church of the Canyons
Canyon Country, California
who explored with me the meaning of
being Christian but not yet perfect.

# Contents

## Prologue

# In Search of the Perfect Title

There is more to 1 John than meets the casual eye. On the surface it is a battle cry raised against heresy, a message of assurance to unsure believers, a "love letter" to the Church. Go beneath that surface and the simple becomes complex, the primary becomes profound and the knee-deep safety of the wading pool drops off with all the sharpness of the Continental Shelf.

To get a feel for what the scholars call "Johannine literature" it helps to compare John the apostle with Paul the apostle. John was a mystic; Paul was a keen-minded logician. John felt his way; Paul marched boldly from Point A to Point B, etc. Paul explains what he means; John means what he doesn't always explain.

While searching for a title to this popular (I hope) commentary, there were several obvious choices:

How to Be a Christian and Be Sure of It

How to Be a Christian and Stick With It

How to Be a Christian in Uncertain Times

But the more I studied John's words, the more I felt there

was a deeper message. He was writing to folk who were not really any different from you and me. They were squeezed from every side by a pagan, secular culture, challenged by an unbelieving world that wanted proof, not pontificating. And they were confronted by every kind of mixed theological message, one claiming Christianity is this, another assuring them it is really that.

Some said: "I've got a real problem. No matter how hard I try, I always feel I don't quite measure up to what God wants."

Others said: "No problem. It doesn't matter too much if you make a few mistakes—Christ's blood covers it all."

And still others said: "What problem? Who's running Sunday in the chariot races?"

But all of them struggled with the problem mankind has never managed to solve on its own: how to love one another.

John writes to assure people who are not perfect that the One they trust is perfect enough to bring them to perfection in His own good time. It's the waiting, the growing, the maturing that is hard. It was hard in A.D. 90 and it's even harder today. We live in an age of instant everything. An airliner crashes and the "mini-cam" brings the smoking wreckage into our living room a few minutes later. Suave private eyes solve mind-boggling cases in 60 minutes or less. We begin to wonder. Surely God is more powerful than "Magnum P.I.", "Simon and Simon" or the impeccable anchors of the six o'clock news. Surely He can instantly solve all our problems, remove all our hang-ups and add all the missing touches we know we need.

John knew that "instant perfection" is not part of God's game plan. He also knew that God is light and we have all we need to take the next step of the journey. John knew that God is love and that we are in His process, which is casting out our fear and filling us with Himself.

In short, John has written a brief instructional manual on how to be a Christian without being perfect. For some it will be good news indeed. They will get a new appreciation of why Christianity is a matter of trusting as you do your trying. Others, however, could get the wrong idea and think it's possible to be a Christian without really trying much at all. After all, if we Christians aren't perfect, just forgiven, God isn't going to be too hard on us, is He?

And there is still one other problem. For some, the concept of being a Christian without being perfect may sound heretical. The Bible teaches that Christians are perfect in the theological sense. Their position before Christ is totally righteous, totally redeemed, totally regenerated. Christians belong to Christ and have crucified the flesh (sinful human nature) with its passions and desires (see Gal. 5:24). Christians are to count themselves dead to sin and alive to God in Jesus Christ (see Rom. 6:11). For other scriptural evidence on the believer's perfect position, see Romans 6:2,6; Colossians 3:3; 2 Timothy 2:11; 1 Peter 2:24.

While our position in Christ is a blessed assurance we need to remember at least once a day, there is still the problem of practical living in an imperfect body. Scripture repeatedly speaks of striving after perfection as we go through God's process. As we will see in 1 John, being perfect has little to do with never making a mistake, always saying or doing the right thing, always being spiritual, loving, holy. All these qualities are exactly what God wants for us. But they are destinations, not ports in which we have already arrived. Being perfect in the scriptural sense means maturing, growing, becoming complete. It is our goal set by Christ Himself (see Matt. 5:48) and emphasized by Paul (see 2 Cor. 13:11; Eph. 4:13; Col. 1:28; 2 Tim. 3:16,17).

Actually I believe there is a better title for this book than the one on the cover. I invite you to guess what it is as you read and study. Of course, if you can't wait, turn to the Epilogue and you will know the secret *instantly*. Unfortunately, the other title won't help us much with rushing God's process. He completes no Christians before their time. Meanwhile, John has some encouraging advice.

# 1

# Who Were the Gnostics and Why Was John So Upset with Them?

*They maintain that they have attained to a height beyond every power, and that therefore they are free in every respect to act as they please.*[1]
—Irenaeus, Bishop of Lyons

*I write these things to you who believe in the name of the Son of God so that you may know that you have eternal life.*[2]
—The Apostle John

$I$ magine, if you will, a drama with the following plot:

- You are an important and beloved leader of a certain group of people who look to you for guidance. This group was formed many years ago by a man you knew personally and whom you loved a great deal.
- You know that many people in your group are becoming confused and discouraged. Some are drifting into the wrong kind of attitudes and thinking. They are in danger of straying from the original teachings of the man who founded the group in the first place—the man you would have gladly died for and would die for today.
- You know the chief perpetrators of the confusion are a clever bunch who have infiltrated your ranks and claim they are only trying to "improve things." In reality, they are undermining everything with subtle lies and manipulations of the group's major beliefs and values.
- You know you must work fast. The only hope for your group is for all members to be aware of the real truth and rededicate themselves to living a more disciplined life that will honor the group's original founder. If they don't, the entire group is doomed.
- As the oldest and most respected leader of your group, you know it is up to you to try to warn your people and be sure they understand two things: (1) the key principles that brought the group into exis-

tence; (2) some practical advice on how they can live better and happier lives if they practice these principles on a regular basis.

The above scenario could be the basis for any number of TV dramas or soap operas. At the end of the first century, however, this story actually happened. The hero who had to work fast was John the beloved apostle who wrote a letter that has come to us in the New Testament as 1 John.

## Where and when John wrote his letter

John's Epistle was circulated to Christian churches in and around the city of Ephesus in what was then the Roman province of Asia. Today we know this land as Turkey, and Ephesus is nothing more than some ruins not too far from Constantinople. The date of John's letter was around A.D. 90 when he was nearing 100, a ripe old age by standards then or now. The apostle was the last surviving member of the original Twelve, and he had also outlived Paul, who was martyred by Nero in A.D. 67 or 68.[3]

It is quite likely that John was the last living person to have seen, heard and touched Jesus of Nazareth. He knew that Jesus was far more than a carpenter who became a troublesome itinerant preacher and ran afoul of the establishment. As John said in his Gospel, "These are written that you may believe that Jesus is the Christ, the Son of God, and that by believing you may have life in his name" (John 20:31).

The scholars argue a bit, but many believe John had already written his Gospel before he wrote this first of three letters that found their way into the New Testament. And he would write his Revelation in just a few years, after he had been banished to the Isle of Patmos during the persecution by the Roman Emperor, Domitian.[4] But there was no persecution going on at the time John wrote his first Epistle for general circulation to all the churches in Asia.

## The world was squeezing Christians—hard

Things were fairly quiet in A.D. 90—perhaps too quiet. By this time the Christian Church had many members who were second- and third-generation believers. They had come on the scene 20, 30, 50 years or more after Jesus had lived. They had not known the Lord or any of His immediate followers personally. They couldn't talk about the time Peter had stopped overnight just a few doors away, or when they had actually heard Paul preach in the village synagogue.

So, it was "only natural" for some of the fire and excitement of the early days to have died down. It was "only natural" for the Church to slip into a routine of tradition and habit. The persecutions by Nero in the 60s and the sacking of Jerusalem in A.D. 70 by the Roman legions were a dim memory. Christians were fitting into the society around them and, as Paul had warned in his letter to the Romans, they were being squeezed into the world's mold (see Rom. 12:2, *Phillips*).

And the worldly pagan system of the first century squeezed hard and continually. Sexual immorality that would have made Hugh Hefner blush was the norm. Ephesus was the home of the famed Temple of the Moon Goddess, known to Romans as Diana and to Greeks as Artemis. The temple was staffed by eunuch priests called Megabyzi, who conducted immoral rites featuring priestesses who were, for all practical purposes, prostitutes.

Heraclitus, a first-century Greek scholar and native of Ephesus, was called the "weeping philosopher" because he never smiled. When asked why he kept such a long face, he said it was because he lived in a city where most of the citizens were fit only to be drowned. The morals of the Temple of Diana—easily the most popular place in town—were, according to Heraclitus, "worse than the morals of beasts."[5]

Sexual temptations weren't the only problem about the temple. The city fathers of Ephesus had bestowed on the temple the "right of asylum." Criminals could flee there for safety, and they did so in great numbers. In addition, the temple did a thriving business in charms and idols.[6] Paul's encounter with the idol makers in this same temple caused a wholesale riot, recorded in some detail by Luke in Acts 19. Occult practices were the norm in Ephesus and the temple was a hotbed of this kind of activity.

So, for a Christian to go near the temple meant he could be tempted by prostitutes, accosted by Public Enemy No. 1 or be offered the latest in pagan amulets or other magical charms at cut-rate prices. But why would John worry about Christians hanging around places like the temple? There were several reasons.

First, Christians then were like Christians now—very human, curious and corruptible. Bear in mind that many Christians in Ephesus were Gentiles who had been saved out of paganism and felt a strong pull back to "the old life." John was fatherly and loving, but he was also a realist. He knew there were weaker believers who might sometimes prefer to pray: "Not Thy will, but mine be done."[7]

Second, not a few believers had been influenced by heretic philosophers, generally known as Gnostics, whose teachings included the idea that since the body was evil matter, it didn't make any difference how you lived in that body. Gnostics were the kind who could blithely say, "Have a good day, Lord, and I'll see you again tonight, last thing."[8] In fact, the Gnostics went so far as to say, the more you lived it up the better, because every experience you had—no matter how perverted or immoral—added to your knowledge.[9]

## The Gnostics were clever—and very dangerous

John knew that some Christian believers, especially those inclined toward being a bit intellectual, were buying this ridiculous talk, because Gnostic teachers were smart enough to blend their heresy with the gospel. They didn't try to stamp out Christianity as did the Judaizers who followed Paul from town to town. Instead, they claimed they were only trying to improve Christianity and make it "intellectually respectable."

Gnostic teachings were corrupting, or at least seriously weakening, the ethics and morals of many Christians, but even more serious were the errors Gnostics spread about Jesus Christ. Because of their basic belief in the supremacy of knowledge and the impurity of matter, the Gnostics were sure God would have nothing to do with creating the world.

Making the world, said the Gnostics, was left to the third- or fourth-rate deity described in the Old Testament. But the true God had nothing to do with making anything material, including man, and most certainly the true God would have had nothing to do with becoming a man.

Gnostic denial of the incarnation took two approaches: simple and subtle. The simple approach, called Docetism, said that Jesus never had a real human body. He only *seemed* (from the Greek *dokein*) to be a flesh and blood person; the doctrine taught that actually He was a phantom, purely spiritual in nature, who didn't even leave footprints when he walked in the dust of Palestinian roads.

## Why John was so hard on Cerinthus

The subtle Gnostic approach was far more deceptive. Chief proponent of this view was the Gnostic teacher, Cerinthus, who became an archenemy of John the apostle. One story, shared by Church fathers like Irenaeus and Polycarp, claims that John went to a public bathhouse in Ephesus to bathe, but when he saw Cerinthus he cried, "Let us fly, lest even the bath fall on us, because Cerinthus, the enemy of the truth is within."[10]

Why was the great "Apostle of Love" so hard on poor old Cerinthus? Let us take a look at Cerinthus's teachings and see:

- Jesus was born a natural man and was especially obedient to God.
- At Jesus' baptism "the Christ" descended on Him in the shape of a dove.
- After the baptism and having "the Christ" descend on Him, Jesus preached with power and told listeners new and unheard-of knowledge concerning the Father in heaven.
- Just before the crucifixion, "the Christ" withdrew from Jesus and returned to heaven. Only the man, Jesus, suffered, died and *rose again* while the divine Christ remained removed from all suffering.

It is not too hard to understand why Cerinthus got a hearing from many Christians, especially the would-be intellectual types. The Gospel accounts of Jesus' baptism mention the Holy Spirit descending on Jesus like a dove (see Matt. 3:13,16; Mark 1:9-11; Luke 3:21,22). Jesus' teaching did contain a new and fascinating message about the heavenly Father and the Kingdom of God. And Jesus did cry out from the cross, "My God, my God, why hast thou forsaken me?" (see Mark 15:34, *KJV*).

But the most appealing part of Cerinthus's teachings *was that he did not deny the resurrection of Jesus.* The resurrection was the very backbone of Christianity. How then, could Cerinthus be wrong?

Very easily, said John, who saw very clearly how Cerinthus was twisting the facts of Scripture. For example, while three of the Gospels testify that the Holy Spirit descended upon Jesus at His baptism, there is no scriptural evidence that the Spirit "left" Jesus before His crucifixion. As for Jesus' words from the cross, "My God, my God, why hast thou forsaken me?", this was the agonized cry of the Son as He bore the guilt of the world's sin.

On the cross, "Jesus was made *sin* for us (see 2 Cor. 5:21); and in paying the penalty as the sinner's substitute, He was accursed of God (see Gal. 3:13). God as Father did not forsake Him (see Luke 23:46); but God as Judge had to be separated from Him if He was to experience spiritual death in the place of sinful men."[11]

John knew that the Word—part of the eternal Trinity—had become flesh and had come to dwell among men (see John 1:14). John realized that unless God had become fully man in Jesus Christ the crucifixion had done nothing for anyone. For Jesus' death to be a once-for-all sacrifice for all men for all times [see Heb. 10:10], God had to be identified completely with man, and this is what happened on the cross. As an early Church father said of Jesus Christ, "He became what we are to make us what He is."[12]

To say God became a man to make us what He is is not to say we can become God, as the Mormons claim.[13] When God makes us what He is, He makes us righteous, holy—fit to stand in His presence. The key here is that *God had to make us holy; we could never do it ourselves.* The only way He could accomplish this was to become a man, while still remaining God, and be the once-for-all atoning sacrifice for our sins.

**The Gnostics also taught hedonism and hatred**

Another name for Christ's sacrificial atoning death is *redemption*. All Christians share this redemption, which was accomplished when God paid the price for our sins through the shed blood of His own Son. The most humble or cantankerous Christian is as saved, redeemed and righteous in God's sight as the most godly, spirit-filled giant of the faith. But here, too, the Gnostics twisted Scripture into their own kind of theological pretzel. The very name *Gnostic* was based on the Greek word *gnosis* which meant knowledge or "to know." Gnostic systems of thought came in various flavors and varieties but all Gnostic ideas started with two principles, one of which was Greek, the other, Oriental:

> *One.* The Greek principle claimed that the intellect—man's mind and ability to think—was absolutely supreme. Having faith or practicing any kind of morals or ethics came second to "gaining enlightenment through deeper understanding."
>
> *Two.* The Oriental side of Gnosticism taught that all matter—material things—was absolutely evil. Naturally, this included a person's body.[14] Imprisoned within the body, said the Gnostics, is the spirit which also included a man's mind, his ability to reason. The goal of every Gnostic was to release the spirit from the evil dungeon of the body. And how could the spirit gain its freedom? Through knowledge—very special, esoteric knowledge.

The Gnostic gained his knowledge in at least two major ways: First, he did whatever he liked with his body. The more experiences he had—no matter how perverted or immoral they might be—the more knowledge he obtained for his spirit. By some twist of logic, the Gnostics saw no connection between what a man knew and how he acted. Their views led to two different practices: aestheticism and hedonism. It is fairly safe to guess that aestheticism drew fewer followers. Fasting, celibacy

and other forms of rigid control have never been as popular as
the pursuit of pleasure.

"Let the good times roll" could easily have been the motto
for many Gnostics who did whatever they liked to gratify their
lusts and appetites.[15] They didn't just fall into sin, they jumped.
The Gnostic *bon vivant* could easily be caught praying, "The reason I've got this terrible hangover today is because yesterday I
took your advice and gave no thought for the morrow."[16]

Second, the Gnostic believed he could gain knowledge to
free his spirit from the "prison house" of his body through study,
special initiations and other ceremonies. All this took a great
deal of time, money and mental ability. It is probably fair to say
that the Gnostics as a rule possessed high IQs—at least they
had a knack for the philosophical, theological reasoning that was
necessary for membership in Gnostic groups.

Gnosticism was definitely not for the blue-collar worker.
(One wonders how many carpenters made it into Gnostic
ranks.) It was only natural for Gnosticism to create two levels of
Christianity: the haves and the have nots. Were Christians who
had been influenced by Gnosticism taught to be kind to their less
endowed brothers in Christ? Hardly. Instead they looked down
on them, disdained them and had no fellowship with them. For
them, the concept of *koinonia* was limited only to the members
of their particular club. All others needn't bother to apply—even
though Christ had died for everyone.

It is hard to say which part of the Gnostic heresy bothered
John the most. These would-be "improvers" of Christianity
wanted to make it intellectually respectable enough to match
philosophical swords with the great systems of the day like
Plato, Aristotle and Heraclitus. Tragically, however, they only
succeeded in emasculating the Christian faith and reducing it to
just one more philosophical bag of wind.

Gone was the incarnation, the unique cornerstone of the
Church. Ignored or laughed away were the ethics and morals
that distinguished Christians from the pagan cesspool around
them. And totally destroyed was the Christian fellowship that
was supposed to commune together in one body with Christ as
the head (see 1 Cor. 12). In short, the Gnostic heretics who had

infiltrated the Church were undermining everything John had lived for since those mind-boggling days when he had seen Jesus rise from the dead, give the Great Commission and ascend into heaven.

## Will the "real John" stand up to the Gnostics?

The situation was getting serious. How would John, the last living man to have walked and talked with Jesus Christ, respond to this threat? Because Scripture describes John as "the disciple Jesus loved" and as the one who leaned back against Jesus' breast at the Last Supper (see John 21:20), there has been a tendency down through the centuries for artists to depict the apostle as on the soft and effeminate side. But a brief survey of Scripture, plus testimony from extra-biblical sources, shows this to be something like calling 300-pound, former pro-football tackle Rosy Grier a sissy because he chose needlepoint as a hobby.

From Scripture we can piece together the picture of John belonging to a fairly well-to-do, middle-class Galilean family. That they were fairly well off is implied by the fact that they had servants (see Mark 1:20), and that his mother helped financially support Jesus during His ministry (see Mark 15:40,41). Although John probably didn't attend any rabbinical schools, growing up as he did in this kind of Jewish home undoubtedly meant that he had a thorough religious training.

When Jesus called John and his brother James away from their careers as fishermen working with their father Zebedee, he nicknamed the brothers Boanerges, which means "Sons of Thunder" (Mark 3:17). Whatever Jesus meant by that label, it is doubtful that He saw the two young fishermen as likely candidates to work in a nursery or hospital. If anything, James and John were a little on the rough-edged side and needed gentling.

Sermons and Sunday School lessons make us think that Peter was the one with the big mouth and short temper, but in his youth John had his moments, too. For example, he could be a bigot and once reported to Jesus that he had forbade a man to cast out demons in Jesus' name because he was "not one of us" (Mark 9:38). Perhaps John remembered that scene the first time he ran across the Gnostic claim that "ungifted" folk couldn't be "one of them."

He could be full of anger and lust for vengeance. In Luke 9:54 we see him wanting to call down fire on a Samaritan village because the people didn't welcome Jesus and the other disciples in the fashion John would have liked. And he had a hunger for power. In Mark 10:35-39 we see John and James asking Jesus for special assignments at His right and left hand in glory. At that moment, perhaps the thunder brothers could have been telling God He was too concerned about their salvation and not nearly enough about their welfare.[17]

## John's life was anything but boring

Extra-biblical writings, like those of Tertullian in the second century, report that after ministering in Jerusalem during the first two or three decades of the Church's development, John went to Rome, where he may have seen Peter martyred. Later, probably around A.D. 67, he settled in Ephesus, a major city in Asia Minor where he became the leading apostle of the Christian churches in that territory.[18]

One tradition holds that John was thrown into boiling oil, perhaps during the persecutions by Nero in which Peter died in A.D. 64. John came out of that one unhurt as he did on another occasion when he was supposedly offered poison and the drink became harmless in his hands.[19]

Another tale of tradition that depicts John as anything but fainthearted or shy is known as the story of "St. John and the Robber." A young man whom John had helped win to Christ strayed from the faith and became a chief in a local version of what might today be called the Mafia. When John heard that the young man had turned to a life of crime, he saddled a horse and rode into the mountain stronghold of the bandits. When he saw John riding up the trail, the young chieftain tried to flee. He wanted no part of the "son of thunder." John went after him, caught up to him and convinced him to return home to the Christian fellowship.[20]

How John did all this is not recorded, but whatever happened, the picture is clear. The loving apostle could handle himself in any kind of company. Jesus had tamed the "son of thunder" and brought out the loving side of his nature to balance and control the fiery temper and competitive spirit. The result was a man who could write the Epistle we call 1 John—a dynamic blend of sternness and loving concern. In his actions, in his love for the brethren and in his condemnation of heresy, John was truly the intense apostle.[21]

As we shall learn, 1 John is an intense letter, written by a less-than-perfect man to less-than-perfect Christians who struggled against the temptations and pressures of a pagan society as well as spiritual confusion, doubts and apathy. Does all this sound faintly familiar?

As we shall also discover, John had a great deal to say about how to be a Christian without being perfect. Does this mean John will tell us how to muddle through the spiritual motions as we settle for lukewarm mediocrity? (After all, Lord, nobody's perfect.) Or will the apostle give us reassurance, hope and Spirit-driven determination to let God loose in our lives in a new and powerful way? Let us see.

---

## Notes

1. Irenaeus, *Against Heresies*, 1.13.6. Irenaeus was a church father who lived in the latter part of the second century. His five books on the Gnostics are considered some of the most authoritative ever done. The full title for *Against Heresies* was, *Detection and Overthrow of Falsely-named Knowledge (Gnosis)*.
2. 1 John 5:13.
3. Merrill F. Unger, *Unger's Bible Dictionary* (Chicago: Moody Press, 1957), p. 838.
4. It is easier to date John's Epistles and Gospel than it is the Revelation. There is a general consensus that he wrote his Epistles around A.D. 90 and his Gospel a few years before. See, for example, A. Plummer, *The Epistles of St. John* (Cambridge: The University Press, 1911), p. 34. Plummer, on the other hand dates John's Revelation around A.D. 67-69 when he believes John was exiled to the island of Patmos by Nero. (See Plummer, p. 23) Other scholars opt for the later date with some compelling reasoning. For example, Wilbur M. Smith writes: "The unanimous verdict of the early church was that the Apostle John was banished to the isle of Patmos by the Emperor Domitian (A.D. 81-96); some writers place the exile in the fourteenth year of his reign, A.D. 95." Smith goes on to point out that the book of Revelation was written at a time of great persecution which had to be far-reaching. The persecution under Nero in the 60s and 70s was

confined for the most part to Rome. Also, Domitian was known for banishing men to exile, while Nero was not. Finally, the seven churches mentioned in Revelation, "show a mature development, which could hardly have existed as early as A.D. 65." (See Charles Pfeifer, ed., Old Testament; Everett F. Harrison, ed., New Testament, *Wycliffe Bible Commentary*, [Chicago: Moody Press, 1962], p. 1493.)

5. William Barclay, *The Letters of John and Jude*, Daily Study Bible (Edinburgh: The St. Andrew Press, 1958), p. 147.

6. Alfred Plummer, *The Epistles of St. John* (Cambridge: The University Press, 1911), p. 16-21.

7. Peter DeRosa, *Prayers for Pagans and Hypocrites* (New York: William Morrow & Co., Inc. 1979), p. 52.

8. Ibid., p. 53.

9. Barclay, *The Letters of John and Jude*, p. 12. William Barclay is one of the many scholars who accept the theory that John was writing about heretics who would come under the general label "Gnostic." Other expositors are more cautious and prefer the term "Proto-Gnostic" or "insipient Gnosticism." Full-blown descriptions of Gnostic systems of thought don't appear until the writings of the Church fathers like Irenaeus in the second century. Nonetheless, there is enough similarity between Gnostic ideas and the problem John faced in Ephesus to refer to the heretics he writes about as Gnostics. For more information, see the article on "Gnosticism" by A. F. Walls, Merrill C. Tenney and Steven Barabas, eds., *Zondervan Pictorial Encyclopedia of the Bible*, Vol. 2 (Grand Rapids: Zondervan Publishing House, 1975), pp. 736-739.

10. Later versions of this story included the sensational addition that after John had left the bathhouse it did fall in ruins and Cerinthus was killed. See Plummer, *The Epistles of St. John*, p. 24.

11. Charles R. Pfeifer and Everett F. Harrison, eds., *The Wycliffe Bible Commentary* (Chicago: Moody Press, 1962), p. 983.

12. Barclay, *The Letters of John and Jude*, p. 11.

13. In his *History of the Church of Jesus Christ of Latter-day Saints*, Joseph Smith, Jr., wrote, "Here, then, is eternal life—to know the only wise and true God; and you have got to learn how to be gods yourselves." Quoted in *The Maze of Mormonism* by Dr. Walter Martin (Ventura, CA: Regal Books, 1962), p. 80.

14. Plummer, *The Epistles of St. John*, p. 18.

15. Barclay, *The Letters of John and Jude*, p. 11.

16. DeRosa, *Prayers for Pagans*, p. 108.

17. Ibid., p. 170.

18. William Alexander, *The Epistles of St. John* (New York: A.C. Armstrong and Son, 1901), p. 11.

19. Plummer, *The Epistles of St. John*, p. 22.

20. Ibid., pp. 23, 24.

21. Pfeifer and Harrison, *Wycliffe Bible Commentary*, p. 1463.

# 2
# Is There an Answer to Our *Koinonia* Crisis?

---

*Some have described the church today as suffering a fellowship crisis. As much of the world today carries out an anguished search for love, many accuse the church of being cold, unfriendly, and disinterested.[1]*
—Sue Harville

---

*We proclaim to you what we have seen and heard, so that you also may have fellowship with us. And our fellowship is with the Father and with his Son, Jesus Christ.[2]*
—The Apostle John

With all the background of chapter 1 in mind, it is not too hard for us to picture John the aged apostle in the role of the retired town marshal who must reluctantly buckle on his guns one more time to protect the citizens from the bad guys who are threatening to take over. In this case John's peacemaker is not a Colt .45, but a pen. He knows the power of that pen, however, because he is the only man alive who can write of personally walking and talking with Jesus Christ. And so, like the typical western hero who never wastes many words, John confronts Gnostic heresy head on:

### 1 John 1:1-4

That which was from the beginning, which we have heard, which we have seen with our eyes, which we have looked at and our hands have touched—this we proclaim concerning the Word of life. The life appeared; we have seen it and testify to it, and we proclaim to you the eternal life, which was with the Father and has appeared to us. We proclaim to you what we have seen and heard, so that you also may have fellowship with us. And our fellowship is with the Father and with his Son, Jesus Christ. We write this to make our joy complete.

The first thing that strikes us about the beginning of John's letter is that he just starts right out. He doesn't have time for niceties like salutations because he has too much on his mind.

His children of the faith are in danger as the pagan culture squeezes them from without and the Gnostics spread their philosophical dry rot from within. So, John gets right to it and establishes three basic thoughts in his first paragraph:

- The eternity of Jesus Christ
- The humanity of God in Christ
- And his (John's) absolute authority as an apostolic eyewitness who saw, heard and handled the Person, Jesus Christ.

John's first words are, "That which was from the beginning." Why does John use the word "that"? Is he writing about some *thing* or some *one*? Actually, he is writing about both. He is talking about eternal truth, the "word of life" that became visible in the Man Jesus Christ. This life appeared and John has not only heard it, he has seen it and touched it with his own hands (see v. 1).

## John had literally memorized Jesus

When John talks about "what we have seen with our eyes" he uses a word that means gazing upon someone or something for a long time—long enough to grasp the significance of what you are looking at.[3] John isn't nostalgically saying he has "seen the day of Jesus." John's credentials are a lot more impressive than some vague claim that he lives "somewhere in Galilee" during the years when Jesus fed 5,000 at a time and brought dead people back to life. John was there, on the spot. He gazed upon Jesus, studied Him, memorized Him, if you please, and the message he wants to deliver is as clearly etched in his mind as the Ten Commandments were carved in those two tablets Moses brought down from the mountain.

To clinch his authority to speak, John adds that he has touched—*actually handled*—Jesus Christ in the flesh. We can almost hear the Gnostics gasp over that one. They taught that Jesus was a phantom who didn't even leave footprints. From experience, John knew better. He had leaned back against Jesus' breast at the Last Supper (see John 21:20; 13:25). He quite likely could have been one of those who shook the Master as He slept in the stern of the boat while the storm threatened to drown them all (see Matt. 8:25,26).

And besides, phantoms don't grasp your feet and wash them clean as Jesus did at the Last Supper (see John 13:5). Phantoms don't consume fish and bread with you in picnics on the beach (see John 21:9-14); nor do they ask doubters to take them by their crucified hands and put their fingers in the nail holes to see and feel for themselves—and believe (see John 20:26-28).

As John begins his first Epistle, it is obvious he is thinking of words he wrote earlier in his Gospel: "In the beginning was the Word, and the Word was with God, and the Word was God. The Word became flesh and lived for a while among us. We have seen his glory, the glory of the one and only Son, who came from the Father, full of grace and truth" (John 1:1,14).

At nearly 100 years of age, John had seen it all—several times. Of one thing he was completely sure: In Jesus Christ God had become man and walked the earth. He had heard Him preach matchless sermons never heard before or since; he had seen Him walk on water, heal the sick, raise the dead and feed thousands at one time with a few small fish and tiny loaves. And he had touched Him, not only at the Last Supper in the upper room, but out on the dusty roads of Palestine as they trudged from town to town.

## The real question never changes

Down through the centuries, the real question has always been the same: "Who—and what—is Jesus Christ?"

Was He a carpenter who hit it big as a traveling evangelist? A healer whose patients never had to wait for results, or who never had recurrences of their problems as soon as they left the meeting?

Or was He more?

The Jehovah's Witnesses say no. They teach that Jesus Christ was a created creature, that He was Michael the archangel who came to earth, stripped of his angelic nature, to become only a man.[4]

The Mormons say no. Their teachings deny the Trinity and the Virgin birth of Christ.[5]

The battles go on. In almost every century the person and work of Jesus Christ has been changed, twisted and warped by various groups that Paul described when he warned the Corinthian Church against accepting counterfeit christs that would be taught by men who would preach "a Jesus other than the Jesus we preached" (2 Cor. 11:4). Forerunners to all of this heresy were the Gnostics who apparently were active in the very first years of the Christian Church's existence.

## John's three most important words

No wonder, then, that John's words practically tumble out as he refutes the primary Gnostic heresy, which claimed God really didn't become a man. And in his very next breath, John moves to correct another Gnostic lie that asserted that true Christianity was for the select few, an intellectual elite who could take the time to study the "deep Gnostic truths."

"We repeat, we really saw and heard what we are now writing to you about," says John. "We want you to be with us in this-in this fellowship with the Father, and Jesus Christ his Son. We write and tell you about it, so that our joy may be complete" (1 John 1:3-4, *Phillips*).

John's invitation of fellowship to all Christians is as broad as the Gnostic rules were narrow. Everyone is welcome, no one is left out. What else would you expect from the pen of the one who had also written, "For God so loved the world that he gave his one and only Son, that whoever believes in him shall not perish but have eternal life" (John 3:16)?

Any study of 1 John eventually has to come to grips with three key words or themes the apostle emphasizes throughout his letter:

LOVE    KNOW    FELLOWSHIP

John wants his readers to feel the great and awesome love of God he had experienced one-on-one to such an extent he could call himself (without conceit) "the disciple Jesus loved." And along with God's love, John wants his "little children" to be sure about their faith. It doesn't help to get good news about the love of God unless you can be sure that good news is true. John is quite sure it was true. He has been there—an eye, ear and hand witness, so to speak. He wants to shout it from the housetops because he *knows!*

And why the housetops? So everybody can know and share the good news. That's what fellowship *(koinonia)* is all about: sharing and celebrating something you have in common. What Christians have in common is Jesus the Christ—God incarnate as John put it, and their fellowship is not only with the Son but with the Father as well (see 1 John 1:3).

The concept of *koinonia* is taught throughout the New Testament, particularly in the writings of Paul. Its most intimate illustration is communion (see 1 Cor. 10:16) where believers eat the bread and drink from the cup in memory of Christ's redemptive work on the cross. Other demonstrations of *koinonia* in the New Testament include: (1) the sharing of natural goods or money; (2) sharing in the work of the gospel and suffering for His sake; (3) close association (relationships) among believers. A brief look at each of these areas reveals how all of them are (or should be) part of the Christian experience today:

*Koinonia is giving.* Perhaps no part of the typical worship service is maligned, joked about or resented more than the "offering." But giving was as natural as breathing in the New Testament Church. Even in the Corinthian Church, a hotbed of carnality, strife and rebellion, Paul could write about their service and generosity to others and how other Christians could "praise God for the obedience that accompanies your confession of the gospel of Christ, and for your generosity in sharing with them and with everyone else" (2 Cor. 9:13).

While giving is a basic for all Christians, we need to remember it is no guarantee of true *koinonia.* You can drop something in the plate (you can even drop a *lot* in the plate) and still not have to really get involved with others. To put it another way, giving—sharing goods or money with other Christians—can be a beautiful way to enjoy true *koinonia,* or it can be a sham, a pious mask to wear while you "buy about $3.00 worth of God"[7] (see Rom. 15:25-29; 2 Cor. 8:1-7; Heb. 13:16).

*Koinonia is serving together.* Moving up the scale of involvement, we consider the joy of joining other Christians in ministry. Recently I visited Westside Baptist Church in Omaha, Nebraska, pastored by Calvin Miller (author of *The Singer Trilogy, The Table of Inwardness, A Hunger for Meaning* and many other fine books). It was a Monday, and that evening I joined Calvin and his company of committed callers who were being briefed for their weekly sortie into the neighborhoods of Omaha to call on people who had visited the church the prior Sunday and expressed interest.

The room was full of anticipation and an air of excitement that reminded me somewhat of a football locker room before kick off. People smiled, laughed, shared experiences, blessings, prayer requests. Calvin led his team in going over a few "plays" (Scripture verses they might want to mention to those they visited that evening), and then they all filed out to share what they had already been sharing—their fellowship in Christ.

"Visitation night" is just one way to experience *koinonia* while serving together. Anyone who gets involved in a church knows the "fellowship of service"—in Sunday School, Vacation Bible School, on building committees, work parties, youth groups, elder boards, etc. This kind of *koinonia* is described when Paul writes to Philemon, "I pray that you may be active in sharing your faith" (Philem. 6) or when he tells the Corinthians, "For we are God's fellow workers" (1 Cor. 3:9).

Fellowship in service is everywhere in the book of Acts. In Acts 15, for example, we see the apostles and elders of the church in action, settling a dispute between Jewish and Gentile believers. The result is a letter spelling out a compromise which the people read and find encouraging (see Acts 15:23-29,31).

Repeatedly, the New Testament shows believers fellowshipping in the work of the gospel, knowing disappointment, frustration, anger, pain and suffering. They also know love, compassion, teamwork, victory and joy. Fellowship in service is a path to real *koinonia* for everyone willing to walk it.

*Koinonia is loving one another.* Today's Christian leaders and theologians cite different crises that face the Church at the end of the twentieth century. Francis Schaeffer warned that "we

who hold to historic Christianity are now an absolute minority."[8]
Jerry Falwell has chosen to push for a "moral majority" in a day
of declining ethics and morality throughout America. Other
major problems could be listed, but what about fellowship?
Could a fellowship crisis really be our greatest problem? If not,
why are so many church members so disillusioned and disenchanted, thirsting for opportunities to really share their needs,
questions and hearts with one another?

In his best-seller *Megatrends,* John Naisbitt describes a trend
he calls "high tech vs. high touch." As our society becomes
more computerized and electronically linked, people have
tended to group more closely together rather than remain iso-
lated in individual cubicles watching their TV and CRT screens.
Naisbitt contends that people like people, not machines, and it is
no wonder that shopping malls are "the third most frequented
space in our lives, following home and work place."[9]

Naisbitt's insights have special significance to all Christians.
The indwelling Holy Spirit in every believer creates an insatiable
hunger for "high touch" with others in God's family. "Blessed be
the tie that binds" is much more than a well-worn chorus from
the past. It is the Christian answer to the loneliness and alienation what comes from a high-tech existence that leaves little
room for knowing God or one another. Naisbitt's prophetic
words strike a note of irony for the follower of Christ when he
writes: "We must learn to balance the material wonders of tech-
nology with the spiritual demands of our human nature."[10]

The reason irony may rear its leering head in many churches
is that they are full of imperfect Christians who feel anything but
balanced. There is often the lack of real love for one another,
disunity that causes division and conflict, disagreement over
purpose and goals, superficial relationships, and little by way of
commitment, participation, enthusiasm or joy.[11] What can a
church do about a fellowship crisis that could include some, all,
or even more than these problems? A great deal, indeed.

### *Koinonia* in a church of 500,000!?
According to statistics released in 1986, Dr. Paul Cho, pastor of the Full Gospel Central Church in Seoul, Korea, had a con-

gregation of 500,000 members, the largest in the world. Despite these incredibly large numbers, *koinonia* is emphasized in Cho's church.

In his book *Successful Home Cell Groups*, Dr. Cho explains how he combats feelings of alienation and loneliness in a church of 500,000. The answer is "home cell groups" which break the massive congregation down into small units consisting of no more than 15 families. In these cell groups, people are no longer numbers, they are individuals sharing in the gifts of the spirit and enjoying loving relationships with other believers. In short, they have opportunity to know the true meaning of *koinonia.*

Paul Cho's ideas are being used with excellent results in the United States. In Portland, Oregon, for example, the Reverend Dale Galloway started with himself and his wife, Margi, in 1972 and built the New Hope Community Church to a congregation of almost 4,000 by 1985. A key to this incredible growth was the use of home cell units Galloway chose to call "tender loving care groups."

New Hope Community Church has already developed lay pastors and assistant lay pastors to minister in over 300 TLC groups throughout the greater metropolitan Portland area. By breaking down his huge congregation into TLC groups, Galloway follows one of his primary principles for inspiring and motivating people: "A good leader is not one who can do the work of ten people, but one who can get ten people to do the work of ten. I get a great deal of satisfaction out of making other people successful."[13]

Cho and Galloway are two impressive examples of how cell groups create *koinonia* in huge congregations. But it's happening elsewhere—in smaller churches everywhere. *Every church needs koinonia,* whether it has 50 members, 500, 5,000 or 500,000. And *koinonia is possible* if believers are given the opportunity to share what they all have in common—Jesus Christ.

### Are John's words relevant for victims of future shock?

As we study God's Word, we are always eager to know, "How can I apply what I am reading to my own life today?" The first four verses of John's Epistle leave no doubt of his relevancy for us. If John were writing his letter today he would make no changes in his opening paragraph. Pagan cultures squeeze Christians on every side; heresies and cults abound; factions and classes of spirituality and super spirituality still exist. Loneliness and plastic fellowship gnaw at the souls of many who seek honest, open relationships in true *koinonia*.

In fact, John's opening words are doubly meaningful to the imperfect Christian who struggles with "future shock," computers that aren't always "user friendly," and a sinful human nature that must be tamed in the lifelong process called sanctification. John has seen, heard and touched the truth and he wants us to know it. Why? So we can make our joy complete as we celebrate our fellowship with Christ and one another. The rest of John's letter will tell us why and how we can do just that.

## *Test Your Faith*

### What Is Your Fellowship Quotient?

Christians in many churches live lonely, spiritually-impoverished lives because their Christian experience includes little more than a once-a-week stop in the back pew to hear the sermon, then leave. Or they may plop in front of the TV to hear the latest word from an electronic preacher.

Others try "having Christian fellowship" in Sunday School classes, socials, Bible studies, etc. Some succeed in finding that elusive feeling of really being part of things and cared for; others do not. Why do we struggle with what should be one of the most natural processes in our Christian experience?

The following quiz may help you identify your degree of commitment and ability to have good fellowship with other Christians. On the lines provided put the letter of the statement that best describes your attitude or feeling. (Scoring on page 38.)

_____ 1. You read about a Valentine social for the entire church in your Sunday bulletin. Your first reaction is:

    a. Circle the date. We'll have a great time.
    b. I wonder if "so and so" will be going?
    c. It will probably be boring.

_____ 2. You are asked to serve in Vacation Bible School, which will last two weeks. You have the time, several jobs are available and you can choose the amount of difficulty and involvement. Your response is:

    a. They can count on me. I love being with the kids and the other workers.
    b. Can't they get someone else? I'll do it, but only because they need me.
    c. That's not for me. I don't want to tie myself up every morning for two whole weeks.

_____ 3. You meet the new couple who just joined the church. They both seem a bit aloof and distant. You decide to:

    a. Be friendly and really interested. Make a mental note to invite them over to your next get-together.
    b. Make an honest effort at pleasant conversation, but have doubts about how you can develop further contacts.
    c. Be polite, but decide to have as little as possible to do with them.

_____ 4. You are quite sure you are:

    a. Naturally friendly
    b. Cordial, but cautious
    c. Suspicious and hostile.

_____ 5. When there is a choice between attending a church service or a non-church event, you:

    a. Go to church, if at all possible
    b. Go to church, if it's convenient
    c. Go to church, if the other event isn't more interesting.

_____ 6. As a rule, you:

    a. Develop a growing network of friends and acquaintances
    b. Occasionally try to develop a new relationship
    c. Spend time with the same people.

_____ 7. The word *fellowship* says to you:

    a. Genuine warm experience
    b. Helpful, usually interesting
    c. Boring and plastic.

_____ 8. In a typical situation where someone in the church is accused or gossiped about, do you:

    a. Keep an open mind and refuse to comment until you have the facts?
    b. Express regret, but accept the statement as possibly true?
    c. Quickly call your friends "to pray about it?"

To find your "fellowship quotient," give yourself 5 points for each *a* answer; 3 points for each *b* answer; and 1 point for each *c* answer. A total of 30-40 points is excellent; 20-29, not bad, but you need some improvement; 19 and below, you have a fellowship crisis. You may want to talk with your pastor, elder or other spiritual leader about your score.

Here are some suggestions for building more *koinonia* into your own life.

1. Write a letter to two friends, one a Christian and the other a nonbeliever. Answer the question, "Who and what is Jesus Christ to me?"

2. John saw, heard and even touched Jesus Christ. He was sure Christ was God. How are you sure Christ is God? What part does seeing, hearing and touching other Christians have to do with your convictions?

3. What steps can you take in the next week or so to enlarge your fellowship horizons? Which of the following suggestions might prove useful?

   a. Call someone you don't know very well.

   b. Have that same someone over for coffee or lunch.

   c. Take time to write a note of encouragement to your pastor, someone on your board of elders or your deacons.

   d. Make a pact with your spouse to cultivate at least one new friendship with another couple in the coming months. Plan definite steps to bring this about.

---

## Notes

1. Sue Harville, *Reciprocal Living* (Coral Gables, FL: Learning Resource Center, World Team, 1976), p. 4. On an introductory page of *Reciprocal Living*, Harville makes the following acknowledgment: "Harold Alexander of Worldteam prepared the original study which is the basis of this unit. His work, called 'La Mutualite,' was written for use in French-speaking lands. It was later translated into English. My work was to restructure this English translation into the Information Mapped format for publication. Mr. Alexander's work in the area of Christian interrelationships has made a great impact throughout Worldteam and its fields." For further information on Worldteam missions, write to Worldteam, Box 343038, Coral Gables, Florida, 33134.

2. 1 John 1:3.

3. William Barclay, *The Letters of John and Jude,* The Daily Study Bible (Edinburgh: The St. Andrew Press, 1958), p. 27.

4. James Bjornstead, *Counterfeits at Your Door* (Ventura, CA: Regal Books, 1979), chap. 6. Bjornstead documents all of his work from Jehovah's Witnesses publications.

5. Dr. Walter Martin, *The Maze of Mormonism* (Ventura, CA: Regal Books, 1962), chap. 4, pp. 106-130.

6. J. D. Douglas, ed., *The New International Dictionary of the Christian Church* (Grand Rapids: Zondervan Publishing House, 1974), p. 67.

7. Wilbur Rees, *Three Dollars Worth of God* (Valley Forge, PA: Judson Press, 1971).

8. Francis A. Schaeffer, *The Church at the End of the 20th Century* (Downers Grove, IL: Inter-Varsity Press, 1970), p. 29.

9. John Naisbitt, *Megatrends: Ten New Directions Transforming Our Lives* (New York: Warner Books, Inc. 1982), p. 145.

10. Ibid, p. 40.

11. Harville, *Reciprocal Living,* p. 22.

12. Geneva Cobb Iijima, "Dale Galloway: Achiever of Dreams." *Ministries,* Spring, 1985, p. 32.

# 3
# The Light That Never Fails

*He (the Christian) will never think that sin does not matter . . . the nearer he comes to God, the more terrible sin will be to him.*[1]
—*William Barclay*

*But if we are living in the light of God's presence, just as Christ does, then we have wonderful fellowship and joy with each other, and the blood of Jesus his Son cleanses us from every sin.*[2]
—*The Apostle John*

Whenever I read the New Testament Epistles, I'm always fascinated by what these writings must have meant to the people for whom they were intended. How welcome, for example, were Paul's words when he rapped the knuckles of the Corinthians and Galatians? It's doubtful he got rave reviews in those churches, but when Paul wrote to Timothy, it's a good guess the young pastor soaked up every syllable of instruction and encouragement. Peter's letters were also a breath of fresh, cool air to Christians who were feeling the heat of living in the pagan society of Asia Minor in the early 60s of the first century.[3]

And what of John's Epistle, addressed to no one in particular but obviously written to believers who needed at least three things: (1) reassurance and reminding; (2) instructions and warnings; (3) plenty of tender loving care.

We've already identified John's target audience: Christians in and around Ephesus. It was near the end of the first century and Christianity had been around not quite 60 years, long enough, however, for heresy to start rearing its inevitable head. As we've seen, the heretics were called Gnostics—a clever bunch who didn't contradict the gospel as much as they convoluted it. Appealing to their "super knowledge" (*gnosis*), which they claimed came straight from God, the Gnostics were confusing the saints with three heretical teachings:

> *One.* Jesus hadn't really been God because God could never become a man—part of sinful matter.
> *Two.* Sin was beneath the truly spiritual Christian who had risen above such mundane matters as failures and mistakes.

*Three.* Real fellowship with God was for the chosen and knowledgeable few who could reach a certain elite spiritual level. (See "John's Three Tests of the Christian" below.)

## There were no Christian bookstores in A.D. 90

How could the average first-century Christian respond to all this Gnostic "enlightenment"? It was a day of little or no written Scripture. The forming of the scriptural canon was more than 250 years off. There were no Christian bookstores stacked to the ceiling with Bibles, commentaries and every kind of book on Christian faith and practice. There were no *Christianity Today* or *Eternity* magazines coming regularly in the mail, no seminaries with libraries full of the scholarship from hundreds of years of study.

Christians learned their faith by hearing oral teaching done by spiritually-gifted teachers and pastors who had acquired their knowledge in the same way—through the ear gate. The question was, *who* was a legitimate teacher? How could members of a church in one of Ephesus's suburbs really check the insights of Gnostic instructors who seemed so wise, learned and even spiritual? To simply say that "this doesn't sound quite right" wouldn't always do. A person could be accused of clinging to outworn traditions, and besides the new teachers could (and did) claim that their ideas were part of the further truth Jesus promised to His followers through the Holy Spirit (see John 16:13,14).

New Testament scholar F. F. Bruce also identifies another possible weakness that always helps heretics get a foothold. Gnostic doctrine fits right in with the prevailing climate of opinion.[5] After all, it was A.D. 90. The crucifixion and resurrection had happened more than 50 years before. It was time for "new and up-to-date" views if Christianity had any hope of surviving as a religion that respectable and intelligent people could embrace.

Imagine, then, the rejoicing among real, but understandably confused, Christians when John's letter arrives to remind them that he isn't teaching a hand-me-down faith; he is teaching what he has seen, heard and touched. Furthermore, he has a message—not just an opinion—and that message is this:

## 1 John 1:5-10

> This is the message we have heard from him and
> declare to you: God is light; in him there is no dark-
> ness at all. If we claim to have fellowship with him
> yet walk in the darkness, we lie and do not live by
> the truth. But if we walk in the light, as he is in the
> light, we have fellowship with one another, and the
> blood of Jesus, his Son, purifies us from all sin. If we
> claim to be without sin we deceive ourselves and the
> truth is not in us. If we confess our sins, he is faithful
> and just and will forgive us our sins and purify us
> from all unrighteousness. If we claim we have not
> sinned, we make him out to be a liar and his word has
> no place in our lives.

John's goal in this passage is to refute one of three basic
Gnostic errors—their cavalier attitude toward sin, which translated into disobeying God. To prepare this Gnostic heresy for
total dismantling, John states: "God is light; in him there is no
darkness *at all*" (v. 5, italics mine). Notice that John doesn't say
that God is "*a* light" or even "*the* light." John isn't talking about
what God does; he's talking about what God is. John is describing God's very nature, which is holy. Here on the first page of his
letter in three short words, John "lays the foundation for the
Christian ethics of his letter."[6]

## Light and darkness never mix

Throughout Scripture holiness (light) and sin (darkness) are
always incompatible. When John says there is no darkness in
God at all, he is thinking of those who are in darkness—without
Christ, immoral and unfruitful—in short, the Gnostics. Perhaps
John has in mind words written by his colleague, the apostle Paul
to Ephesian Christians many years before:

> For you were once darkness, but now you are light
> in the Lord. Live as children of light (for the fruit of
> the light consists in all goodness, righteousness and

## John's Three Tests of the Christian

John has the false teachings of the Gnostics in mind in almost every sentence of his letter. His goal is to present three different tests to assure Christians while exposing the lies of the heretics. The three tests are:

> Do I obey? (The moral Test)
> Do I love? (The social Test)
> Do I believe? (The doctrinal Test)

John develops these three tests in three different cycles:

### FIRST CYCLE OF TESTS

1:5–2:6—Do I obey? (Light vs. darkness, how to truly know God)

2:7-17—Do I love? (Love vs. hatred, loving God vs. loving the system)

2:18-27—Do I believe? (Christ vs. antichrist, truth vs. error)

### SECOND CYCLE OF TESTS

2:28–3:10—Do I obey? (Righteousness and purity vs. lawlessness and habitual sin)

3:11-24—Do I love? (Love vs. hatred, doing vs. talking)

4:1-6—Do I believe? (Spirit of truth vs. spirit of error)

### THIRD CYCLE OF TESTS

4:7-12—Do I love? (Why God is love, how He perfects His love in us)

4:13-21—Do I believe? Do I love? (To have the Son is to have the Spirit, perfect love drives out fear, to love God you must love your brother)

5:1-6—Do I believe? Do I love? Do I obey? (To be born of God is to love those in His family, obey His commands, and overcome the world.⁴)

Note: The rest of 1 John 5 deals with several "assurances" possessed by all believers (see chaps. 13 and 14 in this book).

truth) and find out what pleases the Lord. Have
nothing to do with the fruitless deeds of darkness,
but rather expose them. For it is shameful even to
mention what the disobedient do in secret. But
everything exposed by the light becomes visible, for
it is light that makes everything visible (Eph. 5:8-
13).

## Truth is more than talk

Having set the Gnostics up, John now proceeds to take apart
their heretical teaching, error by error. First, John refutes the
Gnostic claim of close communion (fellowship) with God. Gnostics liked to say they were elite—that their fellowship with God
was special. But John simply observes that claiming any kind of
fellowship with God while walking in darkness (living in all kinds
of open sin) makes us liars (see v. 6).

And what is the remedy for this kind of sin? Walk in the Light
that never fails, says John, and you will have fellowship with
other Christians while the blood of Jesus Christ, His Son,
cleanses you from all sin (see v. 7). In the dark it is easy to lie
while you talk about truth in abstract terms. Out in the light,
truth becomes a matter of morals, not just intellect. Truth is not
something you talk and think about, it is something you do. The
Christian is to *live the truth.*[7]

The Gnostics talked about truth but lived lies. They were
like the hypocrite who has the temerity to say to God, "If my
conscience isn't bothering me, why let it bother you?"[8] The
major reason for the silent Gnostic conscience was that they
mistakenly thought they were above and beyond sin. Because
they believed the body was composed of evil matter, they
thought it made no difference how they acted or what they did.
The spirit was what counted, and for the Gnostics the spirit was
spotless; they claimed there was no sin inherent in their nature.[9]
In other words, even their failures were perfect!

All this sounds suspiciously like semantical sleight of tongue.
The Gnostics seem to join Mary Baker Eddy in her contentions
that "man is incapable of sin, sickness and death."[10]

John doesn't waste a lot of breath on all this. He simply says the Gnostics are fooling themselves. They are so full of lies there is no room for the truth (see v. 8).

On the other hand, the true Christian admits his sins and is always quick to confess (see v. 9). He not only owns up to being a sinner by nature, he keeps short accounts on the particular sins he may commit day by day.

## First John 1:9 is more than a memory verse

First John 1:9 has been memorized by millions of Christians who repeat it faithfully to gain assurance of forgiveness from God. Like many favorite memory verses, it can be repeated without being fully appreciated. Familiarity can breed spiritual dullness.

When we *confess* our sins we agree with God that we have done wrong and we owe Him an apology. But far more is involved than a "please excuse me." Confession comes out of *repentance,* a desire to turn from sin to righteousness. In point of fact, only God can make us righteous whenever we come to His bar of justice.

Nestled in the center of 1 John 1:9 is a phrase we often hurry past in our eagerness to be forgiven and cleansed. God is *faithful and just* to forgive. The concept of God's faithfulness to forgive is easier to grasp. God is always faithful, even when we are not (see 2 Tim. 2:13). Furthermore, He has made a covenant to forgive our wickedness and remember our sins no more (compare Jer. 31:34 with Matt. 26:28 and Heb. 8:10-12).

But the idea that God is "just" to forgive and cleanse us is not as simple. In fact, if God gave us "justice" for our sins, we would be in real trouble. When we do wrong, the concept of justice requires that we pay a penalty. How do we escape the full penalty for sin, which is death? John is thinking of that crucial event that enables God to be just and forgiving at the same time: the Cross. John will develop this more fully in just a verse or two when he speaks of Christ as the "atoning sacrifice" for our sins (see 1 John 2:2). God's wrath against sin, which demands justice, has been satisfied by Christ's death. God sent Christ to take the punishment for our sins and to end God's anger against us. He used Christ's blood and our faith as the means of saving us from His wrath (see Rom 3:25, *TLB*).

In short, the next time we are tempted to blithely rattle off 1 John 1:9, we would do well to stand in awe as we realize that God is being faithful to His promise to forgive us. Not only that, but He still remains just in forgiving us when we don't deserve it, because His Son died for our sins.[11]

With new insights into God's faithfulness and justice, we hurry on in verse 9 to what we have been looking for all the time—forgiveness and cleansing. The Greek word John uses for "forgive" is the same one found in Matthew 6:12, "forgive us our debts." When God forgives, He cancels or excuses our sins, and completely removes the cause of our offense.[12] Why? Because of Christ's atoning sacrifice which covers all our sins for all time.

Finally, God *cleanses* us from all our unrighteousness. Don't fail to notice that the Greek word for "cleanses" is in the active present tense. God *continually* frees us from impurity and makes us spotless. He removes a stain, not just from our record, but also from our very beings.[13]

## Playboys write their own moral code

In verse 10, John makes short work of another Gnostic failure to pass God's test of obedience. As we have seen, the Gnostics denied they had a sinful nature (see v. 8). Naturally enough, they went on to deny they ever committed any acts of real sin. They believed they were so enlightened that their behavior was beyond reproach.

How could they make these claims and engage in pastimes like sexual immorality? By simply using the same reasoning made popular today by the *Playboy* philosophy. The Gnostics decided which acts were sinful and which were not. They didn't commit blatant crimes like murder or robbery. They lived "good, honest lives" and probably even obeyed the speed limit when they took their chariots out for a Sunday drive. Nonetheless, the Gnostics did with their bodies (and the bodies of their lady friends) what was pleasurable. They obeyed society's rules when it was expedient, but they broke God's laws at will in classic playboy fashion.

Playboys, by nature, are concerned with themselves, not others. They justify fornication and adultery with the hypocritical slogan, "As long as nobody gets hurt." When people do get hurt, the playboy moves on to find new fun with some other "consenting adult."

Hugh Hefner, master playboy of them all, claims to have had sexual relationships with hundreds, if not thousands of women (seldom over 24 years of age). He proudly claims he "never got anyone pregnant. No abortions in my whole life." Hefner, who admits being in love "ten or twelve times" claims he is a very normal person who has helped liberate women by "humanizing" them with his legendary centerfolds and countless other photos of nude females. He is hurt by feminists who see *Playboy* magazine as an exploiter of women that depicts them as little more than sex objects. He does have trouble, however, explaining why *Playboy* followed suit with many other soft porn publications like *Penthouse* and started running much more explicit photos. When pressed, Hefner drops any pretense about "morals" and talks business. *Playboy* had to keep up with the competition.

"We were beginning to appear outdated," says Hefner, "so we had to begin imitating the imitators . . . to keep up with, ahh, where contemporary tastes are, at a given time. That's what it's all about. We do the best we can."[14]

As Hefner goes his free-thinking, playboy way doing the "best he can" (to make huge profits) he makes his own rules on right and wrong. What all free thinkers—be they playboys or Gnostics—forget is the meaning of *hamartia* (the Greek word John uses for "sin"). Playboys never worry about missing the mark. They shoot their arrows and then paint the bull's-eye around them. *They* decide what the "mark" will be. God and His standards are never consulted. The Gnostics operated in much the same way; while claiming to be righteous and spiritual, they disobeyed God's laws at will—especially His law of love.

## Everyone sins—even humanists

In the rest of John's letter, the old veteran of spiritual warfare will drive home repeatedly the need to obey God's command to love one another. No human being fulfills that command completely. All of us miss that bull's-eye on God's target. All of us sin, and to label it "mistakes" or "typical human weakness" is to call God a liar. To do that is to be so filled with our own conceit we leave no room for God's Word in our lives (see v. 10). In Psalm 46:10 the Lord says, "Be still, and know that I am God." The Gnostics turned that around and said, "Be easy on us, O Lord. We know that we are good!"

We hear the same line today from secular humanists, who can be found lecturing from their professorships at universities and colleges, making laws in state and national houses of legislation and approving TV programming their studios will produce for the new fall season. All humanists have one driving credo: Given enough time and money, man can remedy anything and accomplish everything. When reminded of all the sin, evil and hatred in the world, they counter with requests for more funds, education and "deeper understanding between peoples."

In *The Finale*, the third volume of his Singer Trilogy, Calvin Miller catches the pathetic dilemma of the humanist with this bit of verse:

> A humanist in choking sea
> Called for help and presently
> Received in full intensity
> Advice. "You must swim if you would be.
> Rescue breeds dependency;
> Self-reliance makes one free."
> "That's nice!"
> He said,
> And floated easily
> And dead.[15]

John knows that the Gnostics are floating easily and dead in the sins they refuse to acknowledge. In just six short verses (1:5-10) John has used the light that never fails to expose the Gnostic error of disobedience to God's moral standards. He has also used that same light to illuminate the path where Christians are to walk as they deal with their own sins.

But is it possible some believers may misunderstand? Could

some Christians think too lightly of sin because all they have to do is "confess and be forgiven"? John will take no chances. His next comments (2:1,2) are critically important, so much so, we will look at them in a separate chapter.

## *Test Your Faith*

This group of questions has been formulated to help you determine if you are currently walking in God's light:

1. Circle the letter that usually applies in each case. A-Always; U-Usually; S-Sometimes; N-Never.

| | |
|---|---|
| I walk in the light. | A  U  S  N |
| I confess my sins. | A  U  S  N |
| I make my own rules. | A  U  S  N |

2. Choose one. To me, "God is light" means:

      a. God is holy.

      b. God is my guide.

      c. God is watching—nothing I do is hidden from Him.

3. Choose one. To "walk in darkness" means:

      a. I sin a lot.

      b. I sin a little.

      c. I do not know Christ.

4. "The better I know God, the more terrible sins become to me." Do you agree or disagree with this statement? Why?

5. What part does repentance (turning the other way from an attitude or action due to a change of mind) play in your confession of sin to God?

     a. A lot
     b. Some
     c. Not sure

6. In this chapter those who practice the "Playboy Philosophy" are accused of deciding which acts are sinful and which are not. Are conservative, born-again Christians ever guilty of the same practice? In what sense?

7. What is wrong with the idea, "It's OK as long as nobody gets hurt"? Could you do a right and godly thing and still cause someone hurt? How?

8. Do Christians take advantage of 1 John 1:9? Do you? What does it mean to take advantage of 1 John 1:9?

9. What does the term *cheap grace* mean to you?

---

## Notes

1. William Barclay, *The Letters of John and Jude,* The Daily Study Bible (Edinburgh: The St. Andrew Press, 1958), p. 35.
2. 1 John 1:7, *The Living Bible.*
3. In his introduction to the first letter to Peter in the *Harper Study Bible,* Harold Lindsell writes: "There is no record of widespread persecution of Christians by the Roman government before the time of Domitian, toward the end of the first century, and Nero's persecution in the 60s was confined to Rome and did not extend to the provinces. The sufferings referred to in this letter, therefore, were those which frequently arose as Christians lived their faith in a pagan and hostile society." Harold Lindsell, ed., *The Harper Study Bible* (New York: Harper & Row Pubs., Inc., 1964), p. 1830.
4. Based on analyses of the three tests in John's Epistle by Robert Law, *The Tests of Life* (Grand Rapids: Baker Book House, 1968), pp. 21-24; and John Stott, *The Epistles of John* (Grand Rapids: Wm. B. Eerdmans Publishing Co., 1960), p. 55.
5. F. F.Bruce, *The Epistles of John* (Grand Rapids: Wm. B. Eerdmans Publishing

Co., 1970), pp. 15, 16.

6. Charles F. Pfeiffer and Everett F. Harrison, eds., *The Wycliffe Bible Commentary* (Chicago: Moody Press, 1962), p. 1467.

7. Barclay, *The Letters of John and Jude*, p. 35.

8. Peter DeRosa, *Prayers for Pagans and Hypocrites* (New York: William Morrow & Co., Inc., 1979), p. 78.

9. Stott, *The Epistles of John*, p. 77.

10. Mary Baker Eddy, *Science and Health with Key to the Scriptures* (Boston, Mass.: The First Church of Christ, Scientist, 1971), p. 475.

11. Stott, *Epistles of John*, p. 78.

12. W. E. Vine, *An Expository Dictionary of New Testament Words* (Old Tappan, NJ: Fleming H. Revell Co., 1981), p. 122.

13. Stott, *Epistles of John*, p. 77.

14. Bella Stumbo, "Hefner on Hefner: 'Real Guy' Is a Very Moral Man," *Los Angeles Times,* part 1, December 28, 1984, p. 18.

15. Calvin Miller, *The Finale* (Downers Grove, IL: Inter-Varsity Press, 1979), p. 59.

# 4
# How to Stay Out of the Shadows

*Christian propitiation . . . is an appeasement of the wrath of God by the love of God through the gift of God. The initiative is not taken by man, nor even by Christ, but by God Himself in sheer, unmerited love.*[1]
—*John Stott*

*[Christ] Himself is the propitiation for our sins; and not for ours only, but also for those of the whole world.*[2]
—*The Apostle John*

Having dealt harshly with the pathetically weak Gnostic view of sin, John sounds a precautionary note for Christians who might think too lightly of their own shortcomings. After all, some might say, if everyone sins, why fight it? Just accept the inevitable and ask for forgiveness when you need it. To nip this kind of thinking in the bud, John inserts a call to holiness. At the same time, he adds an encouraging word for the more sensitive believers who might think they are failures when they happen to fall into sin. To cover both kinds of Christians—and all those in between—John writes:

> ### 1 John 2:1,2
> My dear children, I write this to you so that you will not sin. But if anybody does sin, we have one who speaks to the Father in our defense—Jesus Christ, the Righteous One. He is the atoning sacrifice for our sins, and not only for ours but also for the sins of the whole world.

For the first time (it won't be the last), John uses the term, "dear children." Is he being patronizing or acting superior? Not really. When you are nearly 100 years old and writing to people you dearly love, it's natural enough to call them "children."

## To John, sin is serious business
John wants Christian believers to clearly understand what he

has been saying. There might be those honest but careless Christians who could read 1:8-10 and say, "What's the big deal? Everybody sins, besides all we have to do is confess, be forgiven and go on with our lives." John knows that kind of attitude can turn 1 John 1:9 into a cop-out that leads right into the Gnostic trap. John is saying that sin is serious business. *Never treat it lightly.* John has a horror, hatred and fear of sin that pervades his entire letter.[3]

At the other end of the spectrum, John knows many believers take sin seriously indeed and are well aware they don't go through the day hitting God's bull's-eye every time. How can they obey God's instruction to "not sin" when they know they will because they aren't perfect? Aren't they whipped before they start?

John's immediate answer reassures anxious believers by admitting it is quite possible for Christians to commit acts of sin—that is, to make mistakes. In 2:1, John says if a Christian does sin (one wonders why he didn't say "when"), there is someone who speaks to the Father in his defense—Jesus Christ the Righteous One. Because Christians aren't perfect, God has provided the help they need for daily life as they try, fail and seek to get up and try it again. The Greek word John uses to refer to Jesus is *parakletos,* which some versions translate as "advocate." (See, for example, the *King James Version* or *New American Standard Bible.*) *Parakletos* is the same word John used in describing the Last Supper discourse in his Gospel when Jesus referred to the Holy Spirit—the One who would come to empower and teach His disciples (see John 14:16,26: 15:26; 16:7).

The literal meaning of *parakletos* refers to a person who plays the role of supporter or defender—"one called alongside to help." In today's idiom it could mean "being there for a friend when it counts."[4] Jesus plays the role of advocate or defender every time we sin and need forgiveness and cleansing. We stand as prisoners before God's bar of justice, but Jesus comes to speak in our defense. Like the officer in a military court-martial who defends the accused enlisted man, Jesus is "the prisoner's friend."[5] He makes intercession for us at God's right hand, making sure no charge against God's elect will ever stick (see Rom. 8:33,34; also Heb. 7:25).

## Propitiating God wasn't easy

In verse 2, John gives Jesus' credentials for being our advocate by calling Him the *hilasmos* for our sins. In some translations this Greek word is interpreted "propitiation" (see *KJV* or *NASB*); in other versions the same word is translated "expiation" (see *Revised Standard Version*). *Propitiation* is a theological mouthful that means an act is done *toward God* to placate or pacify His just wrath towards sin. *Expiation* is another theological tongue twister that means an act is done *toward men* to cleanse them from their sins. How can the same word *(hilasmos)* be translated differently in the same verse in different versions of the Bible? It depends on who you want to make the object of the action involved.

Because the Greek construction gives them a choice, some scholars prefer to make man the object being acted upon and translate *hilasmos* as "expiation," which means Christ is the cleanser of our sins. Other scholars prefer to make God the object being acted upon and translate *hilasmos* as "propitiation," which means Christ is the One who placates or appeases God's wrath.

Which do you prefer? To be cleansed from sin is probably more appealing than thinking about placating God's wrath. To say that God needs placating or propitiating may sound to some as if He is a rather unreasonable type who is reluctant to forgive. Bear in mind, however, that calling Christ a propitiation for our sins does not mean He is like the good guy who steps into a disagreement to save a 97-pound weakling from a six-foot-six-inch, 250-pound Black Belt in karate who wants to crunch him for denting his Mercedes in the parking lot.

We have all done much worse than "dent God's Mercedes," but nonetheless He was the originator of the idea to love the world so much that He would send His only begotten Son to die for our sins. "God was reconciling the world to Himself in Christ" (2 Cor. 5:19). God was not only the One being propitiated (placated); He was also the One doing the propitiating as he reached out to offer His pardon to everyone. No race, country or group has an exclusive on Christ's redemptive work. John says Christ's atoning sacrifice was for the sins of the entire world (see v. 2).[6]

## Two ways to look at 1 John 1:5–2:2

Chapter divisions were supposed to be handy devices that Bible translators added many centuries after John and other men of God wrote the books we call the Old and New Testaments. Sometimes, however, the chapter divisions fall in odd places that break up total continuity of thought. Such is the case here. Verses 1 and 2 of chapter 2 quite plainly tie in to verses 5 through 10 of chapter 1.

To recap what John has been saying, his primary goal in writing to Christians of his day is to help separate the sheep (real believers) from the goats (heretics). These heretics (generally known as Gnostics) were guilty of several serious errors:

- They claimed to walk in the light and have fellowship with God, but in truth they walked in darkness, doing as they pleased (see v. 6).
- They claimed they had a sinless nature because their "spiritual knowledge" put them beyond a capacity to sin (see v. 8).
- Right along with their claim of a sinless nature, they maintained that, in fact, they had never sinned at all! (see v. 10).

John wastes no time in refuting these heresies by describing the behavior of true Christians:

- They walk in the light, having fellowship with God and each other while being cleansed from their sins through Christ's blood (see v. 7).
- They confess their sins and are forgiven and cleansed, according to God's faithful promise and perfect justice (see v. 9).
- They try not to sin but trust ultimately in Christ's

atoning work on the cross as well as His continuing
intercession before the heavenly Father (see 2:1,2).

One way to look at 1 John 1:5–2:2 is to say that John is simply describing how to tell the good guys (light) from the bad guys
(darkness). We can finish reading this passage and say, "Whew!
Glad I'm not in the Gnostic camp—it's really dark over there!"

John makes very clear that either we are justified and
redeemed or we are not. That's what he means when he gives
two choices: Walk in darkness or walk in light. But is John writing *only* to show the difference between those who know Christ
and those who don't? John must have something more in mind
when he says the blood of Jesus Christ *cleanses* (present tense)
the Christian from all sin (see v. 7). The Greek word for
"cleanse" or "purify" is *katharizen,* which refers to a continual
ongoing action.

John could have said that if we walk in the light as Christ is in
the light, we know the blood of Jesus has cleansed us from all sin
and our worries are over. But John clearly says that our worries
aren't over. He goes out of his way to tell his readers that God
has provided a means for dealing with their sins, if and when
they commit them.

Another way to look at 1 John 1:5–2:2 is to say that "the
light" meant more to John than being a source of revelation to
show who was saved and who wasn't. As we have seen, light
refers to God's holiness. Anytime God's holiness is involved, so
is our sanctification—our growth as Christians.[7]

True, John has the threat from the Gnostic heretics foremost
in mind throughout his letter. He wants to reassure Christians as
he makes very clear the difference between a true believer and a
counterfeit who claims he believes, but does not. Nonetheless,
John certainly knew that even the holiest Christian needs constant cleansing.

On the night of the Last Supper Jesus had washed John's
feet, as well as those of the other disciples, and said, "A person
who has had a bath needs only to wash his feet; his whole body is
clean" (John 13:10). Jesus was talking about far more than the
fact that walking barefoot in the dusty roads got your feet dirty.

By a "bath" Jesus meant the once-for-all experience of regeneration from sin (see Titus 3:5). And while the bath is a once-for-all experience, every believer needs to "wash his feet" continually to be cleansed of the spots and smudges that come from the defilement of sin.

## Can Christians wander into the shadows?

John's writing style, particularly in his Epistle, doesn't always leave us completely sure of what he meant. But as John Stott puts it, "What is clear is that if we walk in the light, God has made provision to cleanse us from whatever sin would otherwise mar our fellowship with Him or each other."[8]

It's that "marring of fellowship" that bothers us. Those truly born of God know they do not walk in darkness. They also know they should walk in the light. But what about those times when they wander into the shadows?

It is in the shadows where we can play footsy with lukewarm commitment, compromise and sin. The shadows beckon when we are behind schedule on an open stretch of road and the rear-view mirror is empty.

The shadows are so comfortable when a Christian man and woman start exchanging glances, then words, then thoughts and feelings that lead to an inevitable affair that destroys two families.

The shadows are everywhere, even in the Church. In the late 1950s, David Head wrote an amusing little book of "prayers for the natural man" that J. B. Phillips said exposed "with uncanny insight many of our secret wishes and unexpressed desires."[9]

According to Head, if truth be told, our thoughts during worship can be closer to the following than to the Apostles' Creed:

> Lord, give us all the nice feelings this morning. May Thy special blessing be with those who will be active in this service while the rest of us sit still and listen. We pray that we may enjoy the preliminaries, and that the sermon may give us all a glow. I know I have offended at least two people this week with my quick

temper, but please do not let the thought of that intrude on this spiritual feast. Praise God. *Amen.*[10]

Of course, we wouldn't actually pray a prayer like that, but we can slip so easily into its spirit and attitude. Perhaps it's this kind of attitude that contributes to the fellowship crisis we looked at in the last chapter. *Koinonia* is close communion with God and man and, if there is any place where this should happen, it is during worship. Sad to say, the reverse is often true.

## The shadows of the mind

If we are honest, we often do and say one thing and think another. Life in the shadows is often lived in our thoughts when:

- Feeling that flash of satisfaction upon hearing that the pastor's teenage son got nailed for speeding, too
- Wondering if we could have been happier if we had married Jonathan instead of George
- Rejoicing over Marge's gain of 10 pounds on the cruise (which nicely justifies our own "extra bit of weight")
- Secretly celebrating when the church hypocrite gets a "taste of his own medicine"
- Brooding over a slight headache until it is Excedrin-sized enough to keep us from church or Bible study.

The list is endless. We also find the shadows beckoning with sins of omission when we:

- Fail to compliment or encourage someone because we are all wrapped up in our own problems or plans
- Fail to call someone who is hurting because we "don't have time"
- Tell only part of the story to make ourselves look better, more spiritual perhaps?

- Avoid the new neighbors because "they're not our type."

## The shadows seem safe when we think God is angry

It is easy to wander into the shadows when we take sin too lightly. Conversely the shadows seem a safe place to hide when we get trapped by feelings of failure or frustration because our Christian growth seems slow or even imperceptible. We are sure God must be angry with us, as the doubts and discouragement keep mounting. Discouraged Doubters say: "I think I'm a phony, I keep quoting 1 John 1:9 for the same sins. God must be disgusted with me."

Discouraged Doubters are sincere folk. You may know some of them. They understand when they hear someone pray, "I love you, Lord, with all my heart, but parts of me won't cooperate!"[11]

Another kind of personality that hides in the shadows while appearing to walk triumphantly in the light is the Pious Perfectionist. Pious Perfectionists say: "I'm glad Christ is there to be my advocate, but I hope I don't take a lot of His time. A committed, Spirit-filled Christian shouldn't need that much cleansing. After all, it's milk for babies, bread for children and meat for the grown-ups!"

Pious Perfectionists are doomed to disappointment, of course, but they usually go on with a brave front, gritting their spiritual teeth, demanding that the pastor feed them more and more of the Word while they slip further and further into a legalistic rut that may become a grave. Deep inside, however, the shadows lengthen in their souls because they know they aren't making it, but they'll never admit it—to themselves or to God.

There are all kinds of variations on the Discouraged Doubter and the Pious Perfectionist. All of them lead *away* from joy and fellowship with the Father and His Son. No matter how slow my progress toward holiness may seem, it is not for me to cry, "You failure! You can't be much of a Christian!"

## Christians are 10s in God's sight

In God's sight there are not some Christians who are 2s and 3s and others who are 8s and 10s. You are a Christian, a 10 in

God's sight, because He makes you righteous; or you are a zero, walking in darkness, because you do not know Him.

The natural habitat of every Christian is the light. When you received Christ, the light cleansed you from sin in the process called "justification." Now that you know Christ, the light continues cleansing you from sin in the process called "sanctification."

A good illustration of this double application of John's profound statement, "God is light," can be seen in the river that flowed through the ancient city of Damascus. Springing from the rock foundations far below, the river served a double purpose. Where it first entered the city it provided clean water for the city's very life. And then as it flowed on through the city it provided cleansing for the city's sewage and other pollutions. The constant flow of the river gave the city its life and also kept it clean.[12]

God's light is like that river. First, we gain our initial life in Christ when we choose to walk in the light and be redeemed by His shed blood. Second, through the light we gain the continual cleansing we need from the pollution of sin when we happen to wander into the shadows.

In summary, John has told us how to tell the good guys from the bad guys, the saved from the unsaved, those walking in the light and those walking in the darkness. He has told us how we can check ourselves to be sure we are walking in the light and He has also told us to never take our salvation for granted.

Being cleansed at the cross is one thing, but staying clean as we move on from there is another. We can fail, but God's light never does. We stay clean by walking in the light where we can clearly recognize our sins and weaknesses for what they really are. In the shadows it's hard to tell. We can convince ourselves we're in good spiritual shape because we can't clearly see our bulges and blemishes. But out in the light everything becomes clearer. We know God and ourselves better. Nothing is hidden and our fellowship with Him is complete.

## *Test Your Faith*

While most Christians would strive for holiness, at times we may find ourselves and those we love falling "into the shadows." The following are questions to consider in attempting to establish yourself more firmly in God's light:

1. What would you say to a fellow believer who would tell you, "What's the big deal, everybody sins; besides, all we have to do is confess, be forgiven and go on with our lives"?

2. How would you try to encourage a believer who often says, "How can I live to please God? I'm bound to sin—in fact, I do it everyday"?

3. Which concept do you like the best, and why?
   a. "Christ is the propitiation for our sins—that is, He placates or puts away God's wrath."
   b. "Christ is the expiation for our sins—that is, He cleanses us from sin and unrighteousness."

4. Why is it easier to wander into the shadows than to stay in the light? Are the shadows part of the darkness or part of the light?

5. Where and when is it easiest to slip into the shadows?
   a. Thinking wrong thoughts
   b. Failing to be honest
   c. Failing to be loving
   d. Neglecting devotional life
   e. Being too honest (brutal)
   f. Putting things ahead of people
   g. Losing patience
   h. Putting things or people ahead of God
   i. Getting your feelings hurt
   j. Getting discouraged because we aren't perfect

## Notes

1. John Stott, *The Epistles of John* (Grand Rapids: Wm. B. Eerdmans Publishing Co., 1960), p. 88.
2. 1 John 2:2, *New American Standard Version.*
3. Robert Law, *The Tests of Life* (Grand Rapids: Baker Book House, 1968), p. 128.
4. William Barclay, *The Letters of John and Jude,* The Daily Study Bible (Edinburgh: The St. Andrew Press, 1958), p. 45.
5. Ibid. p. 45.
6. Some Christians believe a verse like 1 John 2:2 is an argument for universalism: the concept that everyone will be saved in the end because Christ's death covers everyone's sins whether they believe or not. Other verses that can be used as arguments for universalism include John 3:16; John 12:32; 1 Timothy 2:4; and 2 Corinthians 5:19. There are, however, far too many references in Scripture to God's judgment, which precludes the claim that men do not have to make a choice. See, for example, Matthew 5:25-32; Hebrews 9:27; 2 Peter 2:9; 3:7; Jude 15. The offer of God's pardon is universal, but the choice to accept or reject it is always individual.
7. It may seem like splitting theological hairs, but scholars and commentators on 1 John differ sharply on this point. Robert Law (1860-1919), professor of New Testament Literature and Exegesis at Knox College, Toronto, Canada, believed that by "light" John meant God's revelation of Himself to gain man's salvation, not God's holiness and concern with the Christian's sanctification. For Law, John's purpose in writing his Epistle is not to save Christians from corruption from within but to help them deal with the definite danger that threatens them from without—the insidious teachings of Gnosticism. (See Law, *The Tests of Life,* pp. 26,65.) Other commentators like Henry Alford and John Ebrard, who published commentaries on John's Epistles in the 1860s, believed the cleansing John talks about in 1 John 1:6 and 1:9 refers to the believer's sanctification more than it does his justification. Contemporary scholar John Stott strikes a middle ground believing "light" involves God's holiness as well as His revelation and that Christians must "live not only in honesty, but, at least to some degree, in purity also" (see Stott, *The Epistles of John,* p. 75).
8. Stott, *The Epistles of John,* p. 76.
9. David Head, *He Sent Leanness* (New York: Macmillan Publishing Co., Inc., 1959), taken from the back jacket.
10. Ibid., p. 27.
11. Peter DeRosa, *Prayers for Pagans and Hypocrites* (New York: William Morrow and Co., Inc., 1979), p. 94.
12. Roy L. Laurin, *Life at Its Best* (Chicago: Van Kampen Press, 1946), pp. 38, 39.

# 5

# Do You Know How to Know if You *Really* Know?

*A little knowledge of God is worth more than a great deal of knowledge about Him.[1]*
—*J. I. Packer*

*And how can we be sure that we belong to him? By looking within ourselves: are we really trying to do what he wants us to?[2]*
—*The Apostle John*

P icture, if you will, a TV reporter out on the street with "mini-cam" and microphone ready for action. He approaches a nicely-dressed man who is coming out of First Respectable Community Church and asks, "Excuse me, Sir. We're doing an informal religious survey. Can you tell me how long you have known God and how did you meet Him?"

The man pauses and replies: "Well, I guess I'm one of those people who's always known God. I've been going to church since I was too young to remember. I accepted Christ at age 10 and rededicated my life at least six times during high school. I married a fine Christian girl and we've got three wonderful kids who never miss church. In fact, I just dropped by to encourage my pastor and tell him how much I've appreciated his sermons lately."

"Yes," the TV reporter replies, "but let me ask you another question. How well do you *know* God right now? Do you really feel you *know* Him? What are your criteria?"

"Well, I've always been fortunate to be in a good church. I've heard thousands of biblically solid sermons. I've developed a consistent devotional life, read the Bible through at least once a year. And I've taught Sunday School off and on."

"Very impressive," continues the reporter, "but I still haven't heard you talk about how well you *know* God. Would you say you are on really intimate terms?"

"Look, I've told you—I've known God all my life. I never miss church. I read the Scriptures, I pray, I even *tithe*. I'm sorry, I have to go. I'm late for a Christian committee meeting."

"Thank you, Sir," intones the reporter. "We've been coming to you live, asking the Christian man on the church steps how well he knows God. Obviously, knowing God keeps some people very busy. And now, back to our newsroom."

It would be interesting to be able to transport our TV reporter and "mini-cam" back to the first century and stop the apostle John on the streets of Ephesus to ask him the same question. John had spent 70 years or so getting to know God. He knew all the "right" answers like studying Scripture, going to church, praying . . . but he also knew there is one basic test. As we shall see, this test includes questions that aren't always that easy to answer:

> **1 John 2:3-6**
> We know that we have come to know him if we obey his commands. The man who says, "I know him," but does not do what he commands is a liar, and the truth is not in him. But if anyone obeys his word, God's love is truly made complete in him. This is how we know we are in him: Whoever claims to live in him must walk as Jesus did.

To understand John's Epistle, it helps to remember he writes with the Gnostic threat to Christianity foremost in mind. So all-consuming is this problem for John that he builds his letter around three tests, which he gives in three separate cycles, all designed to assure Christians of their salvation and expose the heretics who don't know God at all (see "John's Three Tests of the Christian," chapter 3).

As he continues with chapter 2 (vv. 3-6), he is still conducting his first test, which exposes the Gnostic moral failure to obey God. He started the test in the last chapter (1:5–2:2) by exposing the woefully weak Gnostic concept of sin, or more precisely, their lack of a concept of sin.

But John is just getting warmed up. He has been using negative examples to show how the Gnostics walk in darkness and don't know God. Now he will use two powerful positive statements that will leave no doubt that the Gnostics and God are total strangers.

## Can I be sure I'm a Christian?
Few Christians deny they have experienced at least one or

more moments when they were unsure of their salvation. John has a simple but profound answer to the question, "How can I be sure I'm a Christian?" We can know (be sure) that we know Him (accept Him as Saviour) if we obey His commands. If we don't obey, we are liars (shades of 1 John 1:6!). But if we obey God's Word, God's love is truly evident in our lives (see v. 5).

In verse 3, John is setting up an idea for knowing God that is distinctively different from the popular views of his day. He knows he is writing to people who have been influenced by Greek thinking, which featured two approaches to getting acquainted with the Almighty.

The Ancient Greek view taught that you can know God through your mind. Plato, who lived hundreds of years before John, is an excellent example of a keen-minded philosopher who believed he knew God through his brilliant intellect.[3]

The "modern Greeks"—those living in New Testament times—believed they could find God through emotions. The "mystery religions" of that day encouraged their followers to work themselves into an ecstatic frenzy of excitement as they watched "passion plays" featuring the suffering, death and resurrection of a pagan god. In this kind of atmosphere, the goal was to get high—to "know God" by feeling Him as they escaped from the humdrum of ordinary life.[4]

There was a third prevalent approach to knowing God in John's society. In opposition to the Greek approaches was the Jewish view, which John knew well from his early training in a Jewish home. For Jews, knowing God came through revelation—the Holy Scripture of the Old Testament.[5] John could undoubtedly remember those long hours when as a boy he studied the Torah.

But John knew there was still more to knowing God. He had been taught by the One who put knowing and loving on the same basis. For the follower of Christ to know is to love and to love is to obey:

> "If you love me, you will obey what I command"
> (John 14:15). "He who does not love me will not
> obey my teaching" (John 14:24). "Now remain in my

love. If you obey my commands, you will remain in my love" (John 15:9-10).

## For Christians, God is no casual acquaintance

It is not hard to understand, then, why John is so firm in saying to know and love God is to obey Him. The intellectuals might say, "I know God" but have no idea of what that should mean in their daily actions. This, in fact, was the error of the Gnostics. As John has already pointed out, they claimed to know and have fellowship with God but did not obey Him. Not only did they disobey Him, they didn't even pay attention to His commands because they weren't concerned about them. To these pseudo intellectuals, John could say, "You think you know God, but you haven't even been introduced."

The emotional Greek could tell John, "I know God. I feel Him inside my very being." But he, too, wouldn't have the foggiest notion of what that meant by way of obedience. To the emotional type, John might say, "Feelings are important. I'm rather big on joy myself. But feelings need a foundation. God is a lot more than a feeling."

And the Jew could say to John, "I know God. I have the Scriptures. And, oh yes, I know all about obedience—my life is centered on obeying God's laws."

To the Jew, John might put it this way: "I know exactly where you're coming from. I've been there and I thought living by the Law was the only way to go. But I met a man who was more than just a man and he showed me the difference between obeying laws and obeying God's commands. I learned that living by the Law is a good way to keep God at a comfortable distance. But obeying commands given personally by Jesus Christ leaves me with no place to hide."

For John, then, answering the question, "How well can you know if you really know God?" is simple, but hardly simplistic. He had met God face to face in Jesus Christ. For John, God was not a carefully reasoned set of postulates, a spiritual high or a list of rules. For John, God was holy—One to be obeyed out of love, not out of grim determination to "make no mistakes."

## What are Christ's commands for Christians?

When John speaks of Christ's commands, which ones does he have in mind? The New Testament lists at least four commands given specifically by Jesus Christ. Two of them are found in Matthew 28:19-20 when Jesus gives the 11 disciples the Great Commission before ascending into heaven. They are: (1) to evangelize—"go and make disciples of all nations, baptizing them in the name of the Father and of the Son and of the Holy Spirit"; (2) to teach—"teaching them to obey everything I have commanded you".[6]

For the other two commandments given by Christ we have to go to John himself. In 1 John 3:23 he will list them together as one command: "To believe in the name of his Son, Jesus Christ, and to love one another."[7]

In verse 6, John caps his test of moral obedience by emphasizing that Jesus Christ is not only someone whose commands you obey, He is someone you spend time with. Actually, He is someone you spend time *in*. How? You must "walk as Jesus did." The Greek word John uses for "to live" is also translated in many versions as "abide." What exactly is involved with abiding in Christ—walking as He walked?

When we think of what Jesus did as He walked this earth, words like *kind, honest, humble, patient, serving, compassionate* and *forgiving* all come to mind. Many other examples could be listed, but there is one important principle to grasp before compiling any exhaustive list of how Jesus walked. To walk as Jesus walked requires active participation.

For example, suppose my neighbor has a huge landscaping project and I tell you I am working with him to get it done before the end of the month. If I say I am working with my neighbor to landscape his yard, what can you rightfully expect me to be doing? You can expect me to be over there with him, digging, shoveling or planting, because that's what my neighbor is doing. You would not expect me to be kicking back in front of my TV set, watching a golf match or a football game.[8]

The point is obvious. Walking as Jesus did means acting in the way He acted. If there is one word that could sum up Jesus' walk during His earthly ministry, that word is love. John is wind-

ing up his first test of the Gnostics. They have miserably failed
God's moral requirements of obedience. Now John will proceed
to spring his trap on another of their errors. The Gnostics, you
will recall, were a very elitist bunch. Not just anyone could join
their spiritual club, and gaining membership took all kinds of time
and study.

The Gnostics divided men into three classifications: the
*sarkic* (from the Greek *sarx,* referring to flesh, body); the *psychic;* and the *pneumatic* (from the Greek *pneumatikos,* referring
to spiritual). The Gnostics believed that *sarkics* were doomed
heathen, earthly men condemned to perish with all that was
material. *Sarkics* stood in direct opposition to *pneumatics,* truly
spiritual men who were capable of redemption. In the middle
was the third group—the *psychics*—who weren't much better
than the *sarkics,* but who had a chance to rise to *pneumatic* level
if they made the right choices.

Gnostics believed that all three elements—*sarkic, psychic*
and *pneumatic*—were in every man at birth, but one element
predominated in determining that man's classification. The
Gnostics who had infiltrated the Church saw the mass of ordinary Christians as *psychics* and a target for their missionary
efforts. Through long, hard study, perhaps a select few among
the *psychics* could rise to the level of *pneumatic:* truly spiritual
ones who understood their basic goal in life, which was the
release of the spirit from the evil, contaminated body.[9]

Naturally, many of the ordinary Christians didn't understand
all this philosophical jargon and they didn't respond too enthusi-
astically to Gnostic "evangelistic" efforts to raise them from the
*psychic* level to the *pneumatic* level. The Gnostics saw these
uncooperative *psychics* as simpleminded folk who weren't much
better off than the heathen *sarkics.*

As the Gnostics increased their influence in the Church, it created two camps: the "haves" and the "have nots." The "haves"
(Gnostics) held an attitude of contempt or, at best, patronizing disdain toward most of the "have nots." And as they infiltrated the
Church, they spread their unloving poison in subtle ways that
divided the Body of Christ into two camps—one favored by God
and the other not really able to approach Him at all.

If the Gnostics wanted to be honest, they would have had to say, "the mark of true religion is contempt for ordinary man."[10] To counter this blatant attack on the concept of Christian fellowship, John proceeds to say precisely the opposite:

### 1John 2:7-11

Dear friends, I am not writing you a new command but an old one, which you have had since the beginning. This old command is the message you have heard. Yet I am writing you a new command; its truth is seen in him and you, because the darkness is passing and the true light is already shining.

Anyone who claims to be in the light but hates his brother is still in the darkness. Whoever loves his brother lives in the light, and there is nothing in him to make him stumble. But whoever hates his brother is in the darkness and walks around in the darkness; he does not know where he is going, because the darkness has blinded him.

John isn't using double-talk when he refers to "an old command that is really new" (v. 7). The old command is one his readers have heard from the beginning of their Christian walk—to love one another. And this command does have a long history. John could easily refer clear back to the Old Testament in Leviticus 19:18. "Love your neighbor as yourself." But John knows Jesus gave this commandment a new meaning at the Last Supper when He said, "A new commandment I give you: Love one another. As I have loved you, so you must love one another" (John 13:34).

When Jesus called "loving one another" a new commandment, He was giving the concept of love a whole new quality of meaning. His followers were not only to love their neighbor as themselves, they were to love others *more* than themselves—in the same way Christ loved them by being willing to sacrifice His convenience, His comfort and even His life.[11]

And John knows that the new command is being obeyed. Its

truth was seen in Christ and is still being discovered. Not only that, the truth of this command is being seen as it is lived out among Christ's followers (the Gnostic influence notwithstanding). The darkness—sin, hatred and Satan's control—is passing away as the true light—God's love—is penetrating to the farthest reaches of men's hearts (1 John 2:8).

As John had written in his Gospel, "In him appeared life and this life was the light of mankind. The light still shines in the darkness and the darkness has never put it out" (John 1:4,5, *Phillips*).

## Jesus set a new love standard

In Jesus, love took on new and unheard-of dimensions. In Jesus, love reached farther than it ever had before. "Love your neighbor as yourself," a Jewish teaching from the Old Testament, became reality, not a sham. Orthodox Jewish rabbis of Jesus' day mouthed "love your neighbor" but were extremely exclusive in defining who that neighbor was. For them, a neighbor could not be a sinner or a Gentile.

The Rabbis taught, "There is joy in heaven when one sinner is obliterated from the earth."[12] Jesus was the friend of publicans (tax collectors) and sinners (see Matt. 11:19; Luke 7:39). He scandalized the Pharisees by saying He had come to call, not the righteous, but sinners to repentance (see Matt. 9:13). Then Jesus said, "There is more rejoicing in heaven over one sinner *who repents*" (Luke 15:7, italics mine).

The Rabbis taught, "Gentiles were created by God to be fuel for the fires of hell."[13] Jesus said, "But I, when I am lifted up from the earth, will draw all men to myself" (John 12:32). And when Jesus was finally lifted up on the most horrible instrument of torture and execution men could find, He set the standard of love at its pinnacle by saying from the Cross in total agony, "Father, forgive them, for they do not know what they are doing" (Luke 23:34).

We could try to capture Jesus' setting of new standards of love by comparing the skills and standards of a master artist or athlete. Ted Williams brought the art of hitting a baseball to a new level that has yet to be equaled. Rembrandt and Michelangelo brought to painting and sculpture new standards that can only be imitated by artists today. Any game or skill becomes entirely "new" in the hands of a master, but at this point our analogy breaks down. Love is far more than a game or even a skill. It is a way of living for those who seek to obey Christ's word and walk as He walked (review vv. 5,6).

In verses 9 to 11, John finishes springing his trap on the Gnostics. What do they know of love? How are they trying to obey the Master's new/old command?

The questions answer themselves. The Gnostics, self-proclaimed *pneumatics* (truly spiritual ones), claimed to walk in the light, but their disdain (even hatred) for the *psychics* (the ordinary Christians who didn't buy their ideas) exposed their hypocrisy. Believers living in the light could step with a firm tread as they sought to walk as Christ walked (see v. 6), but the Gnostics stumbled and staggered pathetically along. They thought they could see so well, but in truth they were as blind as fish who live in the pitch black depths where light never penetrates. The Gnostics swam in their own ocean of hatred, unaware of an entirely different dimension called love where the light shines brighter and brighter for all who believe.

## Meanwhile, back at First Respectable Church

Again we face a choice. We can read John's letter and take one of two approaches:

We can marvel at the way the venerable apostle exposes those nasty Gnostics for who they really are, and breathe a sigh of relief because John obviously isn't talking about *us*. Safe in our robes of righteousness, we can move along to the six o'clock news or to checking the Dow Jones in the daily paper.

But if we are curious about how John's words might touch us more personally, we can dig a little deeper by asking ourselves:

- How am *I* doing at obeying Christ's commands?
- How is God's love being truly completed in *me?*
- What specific steps am *I* taking to "walk as Jesus did"?

Every Christian has to decide what his/her specific steps will be. We usually don't have to look much farther than where we are walking at the moment.

Chuck Swindoll, master Bible teacher and pastor of a large congregation, recalls a hitch in the Marines that included 18 months in the Orient, mostly on Okinawa. He was 8,000 miles from his wife and family, with lots of free time, and nearby towns full of beautiful women anxious to please any and every need of a healthy, red-blooded marine.

The question was, how could Chuck Swindoll, in his mid-20s and a professing Christian, handle a weekend pass? Staying on base was a possibility, but as any serviceman knows, staying on base all the time is a good way to go a bit crazy. There were legitimate and wholesome activities to do off base; the problem was avoiding the innumerable invitations to "get off base" morally. Swindoll, who admits to being "100-percent human," realized he would have to force his body to behave or he would wind up no different from the typical sex-happy marine on liberty. So, he developed his own program of creative, but clean ways to stay busy.

He recalls: "When walking along the streets, I walked fast. I refused to linger and allow my body to respond to the glaring come-on signals. My eyes looked straight ahead—and sometimes I literally ran to my destination."

He disciplined his mind with intensive reading, memorizing Scripture and prayer. He didn't, however, become a self-righteous recluse. Eventually his "odd" behavior attracted curiosity and he had opportunities to talk about what—actually Who—was motivating him. He found that behind those macho masks were fellow marines longing to be free of their nagging guilt. In Swindoll's words, "Purity won a hearing."[14]

## How do I do with the new/old command?

Staying pure is tough enough; John also mentions the little matter of being loving. We might say to ourselves, of course, I'm not an elitist Gnostic and I'm well aware of how level the ground is at the foot of the Cross, but how am I doing with the new/old command? Is His light shining brighter or dimmer in my life? How can I tell?

What about "hating" my brother? I don't really *hate* anyone (of course), but there *are* certain people at church I don't *like*. Can I drift along, never making an attempt to know and understand these unlikable types better, while I keep on insisting I "love them in the Lord"?

Admittedly, these are meddlesome questions. Any or all of them can turn into a guilt trip, and who needs that? Life is difficult enough.

At this point, we may prefer to file away the meddlesome questions on love versus hate and let them simmer a bit in our subconscious. John will get back to the subject later anyway. As we shall see, those who walk in the light really don't have a choice: For them, love must always be part of the territory.

## Test Your Faith

1. Why is a little knowledge *of* God better than a great deal of knowledge *about* Him?

2. How do you get to know God best?
    a. Through the mind—study of His Word
    b. Through seeing Him in others
    c. Worshiping Him in church
    d. Through prayer
    e. Write your own answer using all or several
      of the above.

3. For me, "walking as Jesus walked" means:

4. John makes it clear that walking as Jesus walked includes His commandment to love others. Are you a loving person?

Take the following test to get some indication of your "Love Quotient." On the line next to each statement put a 4 for *Always,* 3 for *Often,* 2 for *Sometimes,* and 1 for *Occasionally.*

_____ a. I like to see people get ahead and prosper, even when it might be at my expense.

_____ b. I like others for who they are, not for what they can do for me.

_____ c. I don't care who gets the credit.

_____ d. I can praise others or hear them being praised without wanting to "put in some objective criticism just to balance things out."

_____ e. When I meet new people, I tend to try to find things I like, not dislike, about them.

_____ f. I always try to give others their chance to talk, gain attention, etc.

_____ g. I praise and encourage others more than I criticize and put them down.

_____ h. I overlook mistakes made by others instead of making fun or calling attention to the mistakes.

_____ i. I never take people for granted.

_____ j. I am immediately ready to help when people are in trouble, sick, etc.

_____ k. I try to be tactful and not hurt or embarrass others with what I say.

_____ l. I am loyal to others and can keep a confidence.

_____ m. When something comes up, my first question is, "What does God want?" My second question is, "What do others want?" My last question is, "What do I want?"

_____ n. I try to fit in with what's going on rather than take over and do things my way.

_____ o. I am not moody—up one day and down the next.

_____ p. I keep my temper when others disagree with me.

_____ q. I have no trouble saying, "I was wrong, I'm sorry."

_____ r. I have no trouble admitting when I am prejudiced and unfair.

_____ s. I am quick to listen and slow to get angry.

_____ t. I am quick to reconcile with and forgive others.

_____ u. I carry my share of the load.

_____ v. I am willing to carry the load for others when necessary.

Scoring:

78-88—Your LQ is excellent; how is your honesty quotient?

68-77—Your LQ is doing beautifully; but don't relax too much.

48-67—Your LQ is not bad; don't be discouraged.

47 or Below—Your LQ is not doing too well. Time for 1 John 1:9?

## Notes

1. J. I. Packer, *Knowing God* (Downers Grove, IL: Inter-Varsity Press, 1973). p. 21.
2. 1 John 2:3, *The Living Bible.*
3. William Barclay, *The Letters of John and Jude,* Daily Study Bible (Edinburgh: The St. Andrew Press, 1958), p. 49.
4. Ibid., p. 50.
5. Ibid., p. 50.
6. Gene A. Getz, *Sharpening the Focus of the Church* (Chicago: Moody Press, 1974), p. 24.
7. Where and when did Jesus utter these commands? In his Gospel, John recorded Jesus' "Bread of Life" discourse (chap. 6) when He clearly told the crowd they must believe in *Him,* not His miracles. And in the Upper Room, on that last night before His crucifixion, Jesus clearly said, "A new commandment I give you: love one another."
8. For the idea behind this "landscaping illustration," I am indebted to George Manfred Gutzke, *Plain Talk on the Epistles of John* (Grand Rapids: Zondervan

Publishing House, 1977), p. 29.

9. Kurt Rudolph, *Gnosis: The Nature and History of Gnosticism* (San Francisco: Harper & Row Pubs., Inc., 1983), pp. 91, 92, 186.

10. Barclay, *Letters of John and Jude,* p. 14.

11. John Stott, *The Epistles of John* (Grand Rapids: Wm. B. Eerdmans Publishing Co., 1970), p. 93.

12. Barclay, *Letters of John and Jude,* p. 53.

13. Ibid., p. 53.

14. Charles R. Swindoll, *Strengthening Your Grip* (Waco: Word, Inc., 1982), pp. 62, 63.

# 6
# Can You Love God and the Good Life, Too?

*Evangelicals today face the toughest of all religious problems: In what way or degree is Christ relevant to the situation in which the Christian must live? How can a follower of Jesus Christ be "in the world but not of it"? This is the question of Christ and culture.*[1]
—Richard Quebedeaux

*For everything in the world—the cravings of sinful man, the lust of his eyes and the boasting of what he has and does—comes not from the Father but from the world.*[2]
—The Apostle John

For someone who is primarily trying to comfort and assure his Christian flock, John has been talking pretty tough. The harsh words were for the Gnostics, of course, but it's quite possible some of John's Christian readers were getting a bit nervous. There had to be numerous believers who professed to know God but who weren't always obeying Him completely. Some of *us* may identify.

Gentle and fatherly as he is, John must realize he has been coming on a bit strong. Because he doesn't want his target audience of loyal Christians to get the idea he thinks *they* are the phonies who walk in darkness, he decides to pause to tell Christians about the blessings and benefits he sees in their lives. As he reviews who his Christian readers are and what they really have in Christ, he waxes eloquent, almost sounding like a poet:

### 1 John 2:12-14

I write to you, dear children, because your sins have been forgiven on account of his name.

I write to you, fathers, because you have known him who is from the beginning.

I write to you, young men, because you have overcome the evil one.

I write to you, dear children, because you have known the Father.

I write to you, fathers, because you have known him who is from the beginning.

I write to you, young men, because you are strong, and the word of God lives in you, and you have overcome the evil one.

These three verses raise at least two questions: (1) Why does John repeat himself? (2) To whom does John refer when he uses the terms "little children," "fathers" and "young men"? Commentators have developed many theories as to why John duplicates his three-fold encouragement to Christians, but as Bible scholar F. F. Bruce observes, no one has come up with a "completely satisfying explanation."[3]

As for who John meant by children, fathers and young men, the most likely interpretation is that he is referring to different stages of spiritual development in Christians.[4] In each of the three stages, God gives the believer remarkable gifts through Jesus Christ.

## To obey God we need to be on speaking terms

The first gift is forgiveness of sins on account of Christ's name (see v. 12). Forgiveness of sins is the possession of all believers, but it is especially significant to the "children"—babes in Christ (see 1 Pet. 2:2).

To be forgiven in Christ is to know you don't have to trust in your own ability, wisdom or "goodness" to acquire salvation. You are at peace with Him (see Rom. 5:1). He is your Friend (see John 15:15) with whom you have continuous fellowship (see 1 John 1:3). To be forgiven means you can feel comfortable with God. He literally invites you to make yourself at home *in Himself* and enjoy bearing fruit (see John 15:4-7), righteousness (see Phil. 3:9) and being a totally new creation (see 2 Cor. 5:17).

The second gift, says John, belongs to the fathers who "have known him who is from the beginning" (v. 13). The fathers know God in a special way as the unchanging heavenly Father who has slowly changed and matured them over the years.[5] Fathers in the faith are believers who have a communion with God that balances the head and the heart.

On the way to maturity some of us lean toward a cognitive, rational side—overemphasis on the head. We stress knowing God through Bible study and memorization of His Word. We become "good theologians" who know our doctrine. No jot or tittle of the questionable or heretical escapes our eye. God, we say, is reasonable, rational. He also does all things decently and in order, according to three-part outlines.

Everyone isn't a scholar, of course, so it's easy for other

Christians to overdo the emotional side. They try to know God mostly through experience. If we're the emotional type, we need signs, gifts, miracles—*action*. Admittedly, there is something to be said for action. Even the most well-studied cerebral Christian longs for "a little fire to hallow the humdrum,"[6] especially when confronting his own doubts or the doubts of others.

Signs and miraculous answers to prayer can aid flagging faith, but Jesus knew that signs and miracles don't necessarily guarantee that we will know God the way He wants us to. For details, see John's Gospel, chapter 6, which begins with Jesus' feeding the 5,000 and ends with Christ watching the disenchanted crowd streaming away because He has told them how they can eat *real bread*—Himself.

## The witless art of living fast

As always, two extremes suggest the need for a balance point. Remember the TV newscaster in chapter 5? He asked us, "How well do you know God?" Wherever the answer lies, we can't find it in religious activities and busyness, whether we prefer to stress our heads or our hearts. Calvin Miller pinpoints our problem: "The last barrier to full intimacy with the Saviour is hurriedness. Intimacy may not be rushed. To meet with the Son of God takes time. We have learned all too well the witless art of living fast."[7]

From his vantage point of nearly 100 years, John knew well the dangers in the "witless art of living fast." We can engage in this witless art whether we are thinkers or feelers. We can live too fast by dashing off to our next Bible study or seminar. We can also be in too big a hurry to get to our next Christian concert, revival meeting or healing service.

There is nothing Satan enjoys more than helping a Christian be in too big a hurry. Perhaps that could be one reason John saves his description of Christ's third gift for the "young men"— those neither brand new in the faith nor mature and settled. By "young men" John means those who have developed to the point where they can take some of the heat. They are the first line of the Church's defense against attacks like the one being mounted by the Gnostics.[8]

## Would we know Satan if we saw him?

The first time John mentions young men he says they have "overcome the evil one" (v. 13). The second time he mentions them he says they have overcome the evil one and adds that they are strong because the Word of God lives within them (v. 14).

John speaks of Satan's reality with the same certainty as do many other New Testament writers. Peter knew the devil was like a roaring lion, prowling about in search of a tasty meal (see 1 Pet. 5:8). James admonishes us to "resist the devil, and he will flee" (Jas. 4:7).

The Gospels are loaded with Jesus' references to Satan (see Matt. 4:1-11; Mark 4:15; Luke 10:18). So are the writings of Paul (see Eph. 6:12; 2 Cor. 4:4). Of course, Satan has never appreciated getting all this biblical press. He would rather remain anonymous or at least appear to be one of the good guys, as Paul points out in 2 Corinthians 11:14.

C. S. Lewis exposes Satan's strategy beautifully when he has Uncle Screwtape writing to his inexperienced nephew, Wormwood, with advice on how to conceal himself and keep his "patient" (the Christian he is supposed to tempt and destroy) thinking that devils are something out of the funny papers, complete with horns and red tights. Nobody really believes in anything that silly, of course, and the result is just what Satan wants—brushing him off as an unreal, imaginary figure.[9]

For John, Satan is all too real and the apostle wants all believers to be well armed for their battle with him. A sign that we are growing into our "manhood" as Christians is that we can display and use some of the weapons God provides.

The Christian's "armory" is well listed by Paul in Ephesians 6:13-17: The belt of truth, the breastplate of righteousness, shoes of readiness, the shield of faith, the helmet of salvation and the sword of the Spirit—the Word of God. It's an impressive list. Many of us learned it from flannelgraph figures, carefully explained by our Sunday School teachers. But do we qualify today as "young men" who can handle that armor? We must answer carefully. The young men John talks about have "*overcome* the wicked one." The past tense suggests these young soldiers have a won-and-lost record with more wins than losses. This leaves us with some obvious questions:

> • What is our record in the battle with Satan? Do we have more wins than losses?
>
> • Why is it some Christians seem to reach the level of "young men" and even "fathers" after only a few years of knowing Christ (in some cases, a few months)?
>
> • And why do some believers seem to struggle somewhere between spiritual kindergarten and what might be called Christian "adolescence," not growing very much at all, not getting beyond an appetite for warm milk, not really ready to do real battle with the evil one, much less work on knowing God fully?

John knows at least one major cause of all this stunted growth and he tells us about it next:

### 1 John 2:15-17

Do not love the world or anything in the world. If anyone loves the world, the love of the Father is not in him. For everything in the world—the cravings of sinful man, the lust of his eyes and the boasting of what he has and does—comes not from the Father but from the world. The world and its desires pass away, but the man who does the will of God lives forever.

With good reason, John turns from being a poet in verses 12 to 14 to being a preacher in verses 15 to 17. As the Christian makes his or her pilgrimage from child to young adult to mature believer, the route has to pass through the world. "Do not love the world or anything in the world," warns John (v. 15). Obviously, John doesn't mean the teaming mass of human souls that God sent His Son to save, not condemn (see John 3:16,17). The "world" John doesn't want Christians to love is the pagan secular system ruled by Satan. *The New English Bible* says it well: "Do not set your hearts on the godless world" (1 John 2:15).

If we love the system, says John, we don't love God, the very goal he has been discussing since verse 8 of his second chapter. As Jesus put it that day on the mountainside: "No one can serve two masters. Either he will hate the one and love the other, or he will be devoted to the one and despise the other. You cannot serve both God and money" (Matt. 6:24).

## What's so dangerous about the world? Everything!

Like any typical teenager we might ask, "And what's so dangerous about the world? Are you going to lecture me on not being 'worldly'? Doesn't God want us to have *any* fun?" To the last two questions John answers yes and yes.

Yes, he is going to give a short lecture on worldliness, but it won't be exactly what we might expect.

Yes, God wants us to enjoy ourselves, but with real and lasting joy, not a few moments of fleeting fun that can ruin us in the short run or the long.

As for "what's so dangerous" about the world, John lists three perils that cover all facets of human experience:

- The lust of the flesh
- The lust of the eye
- The pride of life.

When we see a phrase like "lust of the flesh" (*KJV* or *NASB*), our first temptation is to call John an old prude who is down on sex. But the better word for lust is "craving" or "desire"—in short, wanting something very badly. As for the word *flesh,* John isn't talking about R-rated movies and a lust *for* flesh, he's talking about the *flesh's lusts.*[10]

The better translation of "lust of the flesh" could be this: strong cravings or desires rising out of our sinful nature—in short, letting our natural appetites get out of control. (See also the *NIV* version used above: "The cravings of sinful man.")

With "lust of the flesh" we see the possibilities of misusing physical appetites for our pleasure. With "lust of the eye" we are considering the misuse of our mental capacities for pleasure. Here is where fantasy can become the devil's playground. Robert Law comments, "The most obvious example under this category—the master-lust of the eye—is covetousness."[11]

The lust of the flesh and the lust of the eye go together like father and son. William Barclay observes that the flesh includes all worldly ambitions, all selfish aims. Lusting in the flesh doesn't necessarily require the gross behavior described by Paul in Romans chapter 1. Anyone, says Barclay, who engages in pleasures that set a bad example that could ruin others, anyone who cares more for using things than loving people, "anyone who has made a god of his own comfort, and of his own ambition, in any part of life, is the servant of the flesh's desire."[12]

In *Flirting with the World*, John White shows how the lust of the flesh can start with the most innocent of interests. His lust centered on books—not trash, but fine literature. He literally had to give away his collection of English classics of the romantic era (including some valuable early editions) because he felt they had come between him and his Lord. White writes, "For a number of years it meant literary abstinence on my part. But in His grace He has restored to me, as a servant, the thing that threatened to be my master."[13]

John also mentions the "pride of life," which is actually a more "social" sin. With the lust of the flesh or the lust of the eye you have a choice. You can indulge alone or with others. But when you want to play around with the "pride of life," you always need partners who can hear, approve and be impressed.

The Greek word John uses here is *alazoneia*, which refers to the egotistical braggart. To indulge in *alazoneia* is to boast of your possessions, and even beyond that, to make claim to accomplishments that aren't even yours. *Alazoneia* is more than subtlely suggested in the TV commercial punch line, "My broker is E. F. Hutton and E. F. Hutton says . . . " as heads spun and necks craned to hear the speaker's next words.[14]

### But what, exactly, is "being worldly"?

John has covered all the bases. If the lusts don't get us, our pride will. The quicksand of worldliness is everywhere; it behooves Christians to step carefully. One basic question remains: What exactly is "worldly"? When am I being worldly and when am I innocently satisfying natural human appetites? One person's worldliness can be another's innocent fun. Who is to say what is worldly?

Christians have been defining worldliness for years. Everyone has his own ideas, depending on his church or other training. "Loving not the world" can mean: not smoking, not drinking, not dancing, not gambling, not playing cards, not playing Monopoly, not using drugs, not using makeup, not being overdressed (or underdressed).

The lists go on and on. The trouble is the lists have little to do with "loving not the world." We can all think of people who obey their long lists of "don'ts" but who still indulge in their own particular "do's" for physical, mental, emotional or aesthetic reasons. We need look no farther than the 250-pound saint who loudly condemns drinking, smoking, premarital sex, etc., while taking the customary third or fourth helping at the dinner table. Or how about the Bible-quoting *bon vivant* who loudly condemns the smoking of pot while sipping port at dinner?

So how can we ever define worldliness? How do we quit straining gnats while we swallow camels? One major clue is to quit looking without—at others—and start looking within—at ourselves. F. F. Bruce observes that worldliness is often defined superficially and that it has little to do with our specific actions or the specific places we visit. Worldliness, says Bruce, "lies in the human heart, in the set of human affections and attitudes."[15]

The trick to defining worldliness is not to get stuck on what someone's actions or behavior looks like, but to ask what motives or attitudes prompt that behavior.

## Worldliness gets high Nielsen ratings

The worldly attitude can be found just about anywhere. We need look no farther than our TV screens, especially on Saturdays and Sundays, the two "most watched" days of the week by people interested in ratings. From 8:00 A.M. to 2:00 P.M. the programming is "kid vid"—cartoons and adventure shows aimed at selling toys, candy, cereal, etc. From 2:00 P.M. to 5:00 P.M. it's "Miller time" and celebrating that "Toyota feeling." The major programming fare is, of course, sports and the major target is the man of the house.[16]

Breweries spend millions, if not billions of dollars, selling "lite," regular and "bullish" brands of suds with clever commercials that are often far more entertaining than the programs they interrupt. But in some cases, the beer ads are anything but "less filling." More and more people are becoming fed up. A May 5, 1985, segment of "60 Minutes" covered the efforts of lobbyists who were fighting for a bill that would ban all beer and wine advertising from TV. A major motivation of those seeking this ban was the number of teenagers who die yearly in auto accidents that involve drunken driving.

The power of TV commercials is evident in the prices networks charge for airtime. An all-time high (to that point) was established in the 1986 Super Bowl broadcast when ABC charged sponsors over 1 million dollars per 60-second spot. If the apostle John lived today, he would turn on a typical TV commercial and probably say, "Exactly what I've been talking about: 'the cravings of sinful man, the lust of his eyes and the boasting of what he has and does'" (v. 16).

There is probably no more potent example of a commercial that catches the spirit of the two lusts and the pride of life better than the one that shows a man pulling up to a stop light in his average-looking sedan. Also stopping at the light is a beautiful, expensively dressed and coiffed blonde in her Cadillac. While the fellow in the lesser car gazes longingly (at the Cadillac, not the blonde), she waits for the light to change, her face registering serenity, self-sufficiency and total success. As inspirational music plays in the background, an announcer drones, "For some, it's a goal—for others, a way of life."

Are the villains in this drama the Cadillac motor car company or owners of Cadillacs? It's not really either one; the villain is the phrase "a way of life." Anytime a car becomes a way of life rather than a basic way to get from one point to another, worldliness is crouching at the door.

## Against the world but still of it?

It's not too hard to spot the attitudes and motivations of the world when they come leaping out at us from our TV screens. Christians can shake their heads over "all those pagans drinking all that beer" but they go right on watching anyway. Roy Laurin's words, written before the advent of TV, have a prophetic ring:

> The Bible tells us that worldliness originates within. It is in our love and desire. It is whatever contradicts the truth of God. It is whatever destroys fellowship with God. It is whatever dulls our spiritual senses. It is whatever takes away our appetite for the Word of God. It is whatever hinders our work for God, and mars our testimony in the world."[17]

I have a feeling John would agree. Let's circle back to verses 12 to 14 and review those possessions belonging to Christians as they make their pilgrimage through life: forgiveness for the children, strength to battle the evil one for the young adults and the calm assurance of knowing God intimately for the older folks. But why do so few of us rarely reach the level of fathers who are mature and really know God? Why is there such a shortage of young adults who don't have the foggiest idea of how to battle the evil one? Why is it that many Christians go on year after year somewhere between spiritual kindergarten and high school?

You have to hand it to John. He's a clever old fellow. He is death on the Gnostics, but always assumes a great deal regarding who a real Christian is and what a real Christian does.

We can see him thinking of the Gnostics as he talks about not loving the world. John knows that if anyone loves the world and does not love the Father it is the Gnostic. The lusts and pride of the world don't come from the Father—they come from the evil, pagan system the Gnostics represent so well.

But did John really think that any of the true Christians reading his letter had any serious problems with the world and its temptations? As is usually the case with John, you can take one of two positions. The first position stresses the idea that John is trying to assure Christians of their salvation, not give them a lot of specific help with sanctification—growing in Christ. This position would stress that by the world John certainly didn't mean Christians. He meant the Gnostics and other unbelieving pagans. Lust of the flesh, lust of the eyes and pride of life are real problems for the unsaved, but they're going to get theirs in the end. They will pass away while the Christians live forever (see v. 17).

The second position would see 1 John 2:15-17 as a warning to Christians to steer clear of what can hinder or even destroy their growth in Christ. After all, John clearly tells his readers to "not love the world." He doesn't say, "Look at those pagans who love the worldly system. Aren't you glad you aren't like that?" We've already seen that John is well aware that Christians can sin (see 1 John 1:8,10; 2:1).

John was surely well aware that few of his readers had reached the status of "father in the faith," and that there were many others who still couldn't qualify as "young men," ready to defeat Satan in out-and-out battle. But, always loving and positive, John sets up the standard. He realizes that many of his readers are a long way from that standard. Many of them are far from perfect but they need encouragement. They might even need a bit of warning and prodding. They need instructions in how to be Christians without being perfect.

Down through the years things haven't changed. If John were here today he might even think they had gotten a bit worse.

After making an exhaustive study of the people who believe they qualify as born-again Bible believers, Richard Quebedeaux wrote *The Worldly Evangelicals,* in which he tried to answer the question: "Has success spoiled America's born-again Christians?" Quebedeaux pointedly observed:

> The evangelicals . . . once a despised minority, are rapidly becoming the respectable (even chic) religious majority, the new religious establishment in America. Let them beware. Historically, since the time of Constantine, whenever the church has become "established"—too popular, too

respectable—corruption and secularism have
become rampant within its ranks ... Christ
demands that His followers pick up their cross and
travel the narrow way that can never be popular. In
many ways, that demand challenges almost all the
values of the wider culture that Christians often take
up as a *compromise* because the way of the Cross is
just too hard.[18]

John would certainly say amen to that. He has set up the target for Christians then and now. The bull's-eye is the will of God.
The world will pass away, but the Christian who keeps aiming at
the center of the target is guaranteed to live forever!

## Test Your Faith

This chapter has dealt with a lot of worldly things Christians
should avoid and even abhor. What can the typical Christian do
to stay watertight as he or she sails through the worldly seas of
society?

Consider the following questions and give careful thought to
your answers. Note that all the questions are constructed on a
"scale of 1 to 10." Circle the number that best approximates
your condition, state of mind and attitude at this time. The
higher the number circled, the more positive your Christian walk
in the world. When you have to circle lower numbers, these are
areas where you will need to do some praying and changing.

1. How important is "achieving success" to my personal happiness? (In this case "achieving success" means having a good job,
a nice home and car, rising in the ranks to a better position and
better pay, etc.)

1    2    3    4    5    6    7    8    9    10

Very important                    Not important

2. To what extent am I counting on my faith and personal walk with God as the source of my happiness?

1   2   3   4   5   6   7   8   9   10

Very little                          Very much

3. I value a Christlike spirit more than money, promotion, prestige, power or possessions:

1   2   3   4   5   6   7   8   9   10

Not really                           Very true
true of me                           of me

4. I know when "enough success is enough":

1   2   3   4   5   6   7   8   9   10

I seem to need                       I am content
more and more                        with where
success                              I am

5. I can delegate responsibility or step aside to let others get credit:

1   2   3   4   5   6   7   8   9   10

Hard to do                           Easy to do

6. I am handling life's pressures and taking positive steps to avoid too much stress and burnout:

1   2   3   4   5   6   7   8   9   10

Overstressed                         Stress under
                                     control

7. My values (what I believe to be truly important) are reflected by my actions:

1   2   3   4   5   6   7   8   9   10

Inconsistent                 Consistent

8. God is at the center of my life:

1   2   3   4   5   6   7   8   9   10

Seldom, if ever           All the time

After taking this test, check your answers with your spouse or a close friend. Does he or she agree with how you see yourself?[19]

---

### Notes

1. Richard Quebedeaux, *The Worldly Evangelicals* (San Francisco: Harper & Row Pubs. Inc., 1978), p. 12.

2. 1 John 2:16.

3. F. F. Bruce, *The Epistles of John* (Grand Rapids: Wm. B. Eerdmans Publishing Company, 1970), p. 57. In the original Greek John uses two verb tenses, first saying "I am writing" and then saying "I have written." William Barclay's solution makes as much sense as any. When John says "I am writing" he is thinking of the very words his pen is putting on paper at the moment plus other things he still plans to say. When John says "I have written" he is thinking of the part of the letter already completed. John is pausing to sum up the goal of his entire letter: ". . . the part which is already written, the part which he is writing, and the part which is still to come . . . all designed to remind Christians of who and whose they are, and what has been done for them." See William Barclay, *The Letters of John and Jude,* Daily Study Bible (Edinburgh: The St. Andrew Press, 1958), pp. 59, 60.

4. This is the view of John Stott, *The Epistles of John* (Grand Rapids: Wm. B. Eerdmans Publishing Co., 1970), p. 96; and Bruce, *The Epistles of John,* p. 58.

5. Stott, *The Epistles of John,* p. 97.

6. Calvin Miller, *A Hunger for Meaning* (Downers Grove, IL: Inter-Varsity Press, 1984), p. 25.

7. ———*The Table of Inwardness* (Downers Grove, IL: Inter-Varsity Press, 1984), p. 35.

8. Bruce, *The Epistles of John,* p. 59.

9. C. S. Lewis, *Screwtape Letters* (West Chicago, IL: Lord and King Associates, Inc. 1976), pp. 45, 46.

10. Charles Pfeiffer, ed., Old Testament, Everett F. Harrison, ed., New Testament, *The Wycliffe Bible Commentary* (Chicago: Moody Press, 1962), p. 1470.

11. Robert Law, *The Tests of Life* (Grand Rapids: Baker Book House, 1968), p. 150.

12. Barclay, *The Letters of John and Jude,* p. 68.

13. John White, *Flirting with the World* (Wheaton: Harold Shaw Publishers, 1982), pp. 39,40.

14. Ironically, charges of fraud were brought against E. F. Hutton in May 1985. To paraphrase the proverb, "The world's pride often takes a fall" (see Prov. 16:18).

15. Bruce, *The Epistles of John,* pp. 60, 61.

16. Brent Bill, *Stay Tuned* (Old Tappan, NJ: Fleming H. Revell, Co., 1985), p. 49.

17. Roy Laurin, *Life at Its Best* (Chicago: Van Kampen Press, 1946), p. 67.

18. Richard Quebedeaux, *The Worldly Evangelicals* (San Francisco: Harper & Row Pubs., Inc., 1978), p. 168.

19. Adapted from Archibald Hart, *The Success Factor* (Old Tappan, NJ: Fleming H. Revell Co., 1984), pp. 20, 21.

# 7
# How to Hold Your Own with the Junior Antichrists

*If Christ is not true God equally with the Father, there is no essential difference between Christianity and pagan polytheism.*[1]
—Dorothy Sayers

*A person who doesn't believe in Christ, God's Son, can't have God the Father either. But he who has Christ, God's Son, has God the Father also.*[2]
—The Apostle John

Question: Who is the only biblical writer who uses the term *antichrist*, and in what books does this word appear?

Answer: John the apostle, four times in 1 John 2:18, 22; 4:3, and once in 2 John 7.

Before filing this tidbit away for your next round of Bible trivia, it might be worth wondering why John mentions the word *antichrist* at all. Would his readers even understand it? After all, it isn't a term used by any other biblical writer, not even Paul.[3]

John's Gentile readers (Christians saved out of Greek paganism) might have been a bit vague on the antichrist, but Jewish Christians were not. The concept of a lawless one of terrible power went all the way back to the prophet Daniel who wrote of the "king of the North" who would desecrate the Temple in Jerusalem and abolish daily sacrifices, setting up the "abomination that causes desolation" (Dan. 11:31). Partial fulfillment of Daniel's prophecy was thought to have occurred when Syrian King Antiochus Epiphanes invaded Jerusalem and desecrated the Temple by sacrificing swine on the altar in 168 B.C. Another partial fulfillment was attributed to Titus, who led the Roman legions in destroying the Temple along with the rest of Jerusalem in A.D. 70.

Why, however, does John bring up the antichrist at this point? As usual, he is thinking of the group that is seldom far from his mind, the Gnostics. So far, John has completed two parts of his first round of tests to assure the Christians and expose the heretics.

In chapter 1, verse 5, through chapter 2, verse 6, John conducted the moral test that revealed the Gnostic's refusal to obey God (see 1:6,8,10). At the same time, John explained how the true Christian handles his own sins (see 1:7,9; 2:1,2).

In chapter 2, verses 4 to 11, John conducted the social test that exposed the Gnostic's elitist attitude and failure to love. At the same time, he reviewed the new/old command that all believers have known and tried to obey from the beginning—to love one another.

In chapter 2, verses 12 to 14, John stopped to reassure Christians by listing the possessions they have in Christ, and in verses 15 to 17 he warned believers against loving the pagan, worldly system and its values.

Now John will complete his first round of tests with some pointed words about doctrine. As usual, his goal is two-fold: (1) to expose the Gnostic heretics; (2) to reassure true Christian believers. And so he confronts the vilest Gnostic heresy of them all: their claim that God could never become a man and, therefore, the incarnation of God in Jesus Christ was a farce. To all this, John replies:

### 1 John 2:18-23

Dear children, this is the last hour; and as you have heard that the antichrist is coming, even now many antichrists have come. This is how we know it is the last hour. They went out from us, but they did not really belong to us. For if they had belonged to us, they would have remained with us; but their going showed that none of them belonged to us.

But you have an anointing from the Holy One, and all of you know the truth. I do not write to you because you do not know the truth, but because you do know it and because no lie comes from the truth. Who is the liar? It is the man who denies that Jesus is the Christ. Such a man is the antichrist—he denies the Father and the Son. No one who denies the Son has the Father; whoever acknowledges the Son has the Father also.

With his first words, John unhesitatingly lumps the Gnostics with the antichrist. In fact, he calls them "little antichrists" who are doing a first class job of opposing Christ in this "last hour,"[4] before the grand finale when the senior man of lawlessness will wreak his havoc.

## How to recognize a "junior antichrist"

How does John identify these "junior antichrists"? They are the Gnostic heretics who have left the fellowship. "If they really belonged to us, they would have stayed," says John, "but now we know who they really are because they deserted the ranks."

John knows, however, that many of these deserters aren't through making trouble. Some of them are still hanging around, trying to spread their false doctrines among any Christians who will listen. On more than one occasion the Gnostic trouble-makers must have reminded John of warnings he heard personally from Jesus Himself:

> For many will come in my name, claiming, "I am the Christ," and will deceive many (Matt. 24:5).

> For false Christs and false prophets will appear and perform great signs and miracles to deceive even the elect (Matt. 24:24).[5]

While John warns his sheep that antichrist wolves are prowling about, he doesn't want them to panic. True Christians have protection—the anointing of the Holy One who helps them know the truth (see v. 20). Here is John's first reference to the Holy Spirit in his Epistle, but it will not be the last. In a way it is not too surprising that John waits until now to mention the anointing *(chrisma)* that every Christian receives at salvation. John wants to remind his children in the faith that they have One sent from Christ who is even more powerful than the antichrist. Their anointing is by, through and from the Counselor whom Jesus promised at the Last Supper when He told John and the other disciples: "The Holy spirit, whom the Father will send in my name, will teach you all things and will remind you of everything I have said to you" (John 14:26).[6]

The King James Version of 1 John 2:20 uses the word "unction," but "anointing" is better because it clearly suggests that the believer has been imparted something. There can be little doubt that the "something" John is referring to is the Holy Spirit because of his strong emphasis in his very next words about believers "knowing the truth." They know the truth through the Holy Spirit whom Christ promised to send (see John 14:26). This must have been especially good news to John's first-century readers, who were being confused by Gnostic teachers who kept insisting, "We have new and special truth straight from God."

## All Christians have the Spirit's anointing

Is John trying to counter Gnostic elitism by setting up some kind of esoteric club of believers who could say, "I'm anointed, are you?" Obviously, John is doing exactly the opposite. He wants all Christians within reach of his letter to know that the gift of the Holy Spirit doesn't depend upon reaching some particular level of spiritual maturity or having a special experience of some kind.[7] *All* Christians receive the gift of the Holy Spirit at the moment of their new birth. John has no trouble agreeing with Paul's letter to Ephesian Christians which clearly states, "You also were included in Christ when you heard the word of truth, the gospel of your salvation. Having believed, you were marked in him with a seal, the promised Holy Spirit" (Eph. 1:13).

John clearly understands that in taking on the Gnostics he is not engaging in mild philosophical debate. In the war with the antichrist, the mind is a literal battleground.[8] He knows that the antichrist is after the very minds and souls of Christian believers. "Brainwashing" may be a twentieth-century term, but it has been going on since time began. John knew that his flock was being brainwashed by Gnostic teachers who tirelessly attempted to indoctrinate Christian believers with their "fresh new insights into truth."

But John also knew that Christians don't need to be taught as much as they need to be reminded.[9] Christians of the first century needed the same advice we need today: "Remember who you are in Jesus Christ!"

John is telling his Christian friends, "Let's not let the Gnostics get us in a muddle. We know that lies don't come out of truth. How can we test these people to see if they're lying? Let's go right back to the bottom line. If they deny that Jesus is the Christ—God Himself—they are working for the antichrist. These Gnostics like to say, 'We may have a few differences on Jesus, but we both know the same God.' But that's a lie, also. If they deny the Son—Jesus Christ—they don't have the Father either!" (see 1 John 2:22,23).

## Meanwhile, back at your own front door

About here, Mr. or Ms. Typical Christian may be yawning a bit and saying, "All this eschatology is fascinating, but does talking about junior antichrists really have much to do with me?"

To reply in the vernacular, "Does catching cold have much to do with a virus?" Twentieth-century versions of the Gnostics are busier than ever running up and down the streets of your neighborhood, ringing doorbells and politely asking to be invited in.

Few people reading this book have not been visited by a couple (it can be two women, two men, a man and a woman, and sometimes a parent and a child) holding a *Watchtower* or an *Awake* in their hands and asking questions about the economy or some other "relevant" subject. The Jehovah's Witnesses are one of the fastest growing cults in the world due to a simple strategy: They know what they believe and they demand unquestioning discipline and obedience from their members, who are carefully schooled and sent out to spread their teaching to anyone who will listen.

To deal effectively with Jehovah's Witnesses, you must be well-versed in what the Scriptures teach about the deity of Christ and His atoning work on the Cross. You also need to know some basics about what the Witnesses teach. Literature on this fast-growing cult is available in every form from brief to voluminous.

One of the best books you can obtain, which will give you excellent information without overwhelming you with facts, is *Counterfeits at Your Door* by James Bjornstad. Bjornstad's book gives excellent helps in knowing the basic doctrine of Jesus' deity, humanity, death and saving sacrifice and resurrection. He also gives actual sample conversations between Christians and

Jehovah's Witnesses to show how to answer the questions they ask and handle their manipulations of Scripture.[10]

Bjornstad is especially helpful with explaining the key to Jehovah's Witness heresy, which concerns the Person of Christ. Similarities between Jehovah's Witness doctrines and Gnostic heresies are evident in many of their teachings:

- The Witnesses claim that Jesus went through three separate states of being: (1) Before He appeared on earth, Jesus was the archangel Michael in heaven; (2) while He was here on earth, Jesus was a man and nothing more; (3) at present Jesus is now back in heaven as the archangel Michael.

- When Witnesses call Jesus "the only begotten Son of God" they mean He is a superior being created directly by God. In addition to referring to Jesus as the archangel Michael, the Jehovah's Witnesses also call Him the Word or Logos, which in their language means "one who speaks for Jehovah."

- The Witnesses grant that Jesus was "miraculously conceived" in the womb of the Virgin Mary when Jehovah took the "life force" of Michael and put it there. When Jesus was born of Mary, He laid aside His spirit existence and became a man, but nothing more.

- Jesus proved to be Jehovah's "chief witness" by living a perfect and sinless life on earth. When He died, His human life was annihilated—blotted out of existence.

- The Witnesses explain Jesus' resurrection by saying He was raised as an "immortal spirit," actually a re-creation to his former state as the archangel Michael. They explain His appearances in bodily form during the 40 days after His resurrection as the same kind of appearance angels make in other scriptural accounts, for example, the visit of two angels to Sodom where Lot invites them to dinner. Jesus is

nothing more than an angel now immortal. He has
continued to be an angel and will remain so forever.

All of the above Jehovah's Witness teachings are documented by James Bjornstad in *Counterfeits at Your Door.*[11] To
sum up their views of the person of Christ, the Jehovah's Witnesses admit that Jesus is superior to all other created beings,
but He is not eternal or co-equal with the Father (Jehovah). As
Bjornstad points out, the Witnesses believe that Jesus "is the
Father's first creation and nothing more—Michael the archangel."[12]

Reviewing the heretical teachings of groups like the Jehovah's Witnesses illustrates the relevancy of what John is saying
in chapter 2 of his letter. While the Gnostics and the Witnesses
are not precisely identical in their teachings, they both sprout
from the same kind of root. Those who deny the incarnation
have been alive and very active since the first days of Christianity. Taking on the Jehovah's Witnesses is a good exercise to see
just how much we really know and understand about the deity of
Christ.

### But is all this doctrine really relevant?

In today's "I gotta be me—I know God wants me to be ful-
filled and happy" atmosphere which has permeated many Christian circles, it is easy to overlook basic doctrines. We tend to
say, "Come on, I know all that stuff about the deity of Christ.
Let's talk about something relevant, like marriage encounter,
signs and wonders or stopping abortion."

Our problem really isn't new. Every generation worries
about being "relevant"—meaning "what's in this for me?" In
1949, Dorothy Sayers, a writer of fiction, who also happened to
be a fine theologian in her own right, penned these lines:

It is not true at all that dogma is "hopelessly irrelevant to the life and thought of the average man . . . .
The central dogma of the incarnation is that by which
relevance stands or falls. If Christ was only man,
then He is entirely irrelevant to any thought about

God; if He is only God, then He is entirely irrelevant
to any experience of human life. It is, in the strictest
sense, necessary . . . that a man should believe
rightly the incarnation of our Lord Jesus Christ.
Unless he believes rightly, there is not the faintest
reason why he should believe at all. [13]

John would have liked Dorothy. His entire Epistle is filled
with admonishments to believe rightly or not at all. It is no mystery that the revered old apostle of love came out swinging at
heresies like those spread by the Gnostics. John knew he was in
no gentlemanly debate on minor points of church policy. He realized that the very fate of the Christian faith was at stake. He
knew that, without the incarnation, any talk of a resurrection
was pointless. John would have also liked the words of Roy
Laurin, contemporary of Dorothy Sayers who wrote:

Why is belief in the incarnation so important? It is
the heart of Christianity. Had there been no incarnation, Christ would have been an *apotheosis*, a man
moving toward God. Christianity would have been
only another approach toward God. Christ would
have been only a godlike man. But there was an
incarnation, *God moved toward man.* Because of
that, Christianity is in reality God's approach to man.
Christ is, in fact, a man-like God. The incarnation is
what makes Christianity distinctly unlike any other
system. A belief not founded on the incarnation is
anti-Christian. [14]

Through the incarnation, God not only moved toward man,
He took up residence within him. That's why John hurries on to
tell Christians how and why they can always be safe from the
harmful teachings of heretics:

**1 John 2:24-27**
See that what you have heard from the beginning
remains in you. If it does, you also will remain in the

Son and in the Father. And this is what he promised us—even eternal life.

I am writing these things to you about those who are trying to lead you astray. As for you, the anointing you received from him remains in you, and you do not need anyone to teach you. But as his anointing teaches you about all things and as that anointing is real, not counterfeit—just as it has taught you, remain in him.

John sums up his third criticism of the Gnostics and his first round of tests by urging his readers to "keep faithful to what you heard at the beginning" (1 John 2:24, *Phillips*). He's not just saying, "Be good little Christians, keep going to church and saying your prayers, and try to read the Scriptures everyday." He wants the Word of God to remain in them—*at the very center of their lives*. If it does, John knows they "also will remain in the Son and in the Father" (v. 24).

John keeps pounding away on certain things like "the message you've heard from the beginning" because he knows how easy it is for believers to neglect or even abuse God's Word. Christians in John's day had the same problems the Church faces today. Christians might doubt—just a little bit—the accuracy and inspiration of the Scriptures. Once they open that door, even a crack, the wolves have a good chance to get in.

In his helpful discussion of discipleship for the long run, *The Race*, author John White observes that today Christians use the term *inspiration* rather loosely. Anyone can get inspired, from a musician to an athlete to a political candidate. Christians have been taught that the Holy Spirit moved men to write the Scriptures, but controlled them in such a way that His revelation came down without errors.

White says: "Some Christians ask, 'How could they be free from error if the inspiration came through imperfect humans?' I do not know. I could, however, ask the same question of Christ. How could He be truly free from sin if He was born of a woman whose life, however good, contained sin? For myself, I only know *what God did*. I do not know *how He did it*. He gave us a living Word, free from sin, and a written Word, free from error."[15]

Believing in the inspiration and inerrancy of Scripture doesn't necessarily do the whole job. As John has already said, we can love the world far more than we should. We can let the pagan system influence our hearts and minds more than God does.

Coping with life's myriad distractions would be impossible except for the Christian's secret weapon—the anointing of the Holy Spirit. John assures his readers that the Holy Spirit is always there, ready to teach them what they need to know—*as long as they are really listening*.

Christians may debate the possibility of a believer losing the Holy Spirit, but Scripture makes it quite clear that you can quench Him (see 1 Thess. 5:19). There are several effective ways to do that, all of which play into the hands of those who want to lead you astray.

One obvious way to quench the Holy Spirit is to not read the Scriptures or pray, two chief ways in which God talks to you.

Another excellent Spirit-quencher is to stay away from other Christians. Don't go to church; don't take part in Bible studies or small groups where you might share your needs and problems and get some help.

Finally, if none of the above seem to work, try playing the game called "going through all the right motions." This is more subtle, but extremely effective with some personalities and temperaments. The idea is to read your Bible several times a week, but don't worry if you "don't get much out of it." Be sure to attend worship regularly, but feel free to turn off the "boring parts that don't quite grab you." Take part in "safe" prayer meetings where there is a lot of talk about "they" and "them" who are "out there," and where there is a great deal of concern about being "blessed and guided in a general way." Avoid, however, getting specific. Avoid thinking about how God's Word should make a practical difference in your life and even *change your comfortable style or routine*. Continue going through the motions, knowing that you are saved, sealed and well on the way to being sanctified.

We know instinctively there is something very wrong with

just going through the motions. We abhor apathy and half-heartedness. Unfortunately, we see faults in others much more clearly than we do in ourselves. What is our best safeguard against spiritual deadness and dry rot that leaves us easy prey for those who want to lead us astray? The answer is to "abide in the truth" or as J. B. Phillips puts it "live continually in him" (1 John 2:27, *Phillips*).

John Stott sums up verses 26 and 27 by saying: "The only safeguard against lies is to have abiding within us both the Word that we have heard from the beginning and the anointing that we have received from Him. It is by these old possessions, not by new teachings or teachers, that we shall abide in the truth."[16]

John knows that if Christians "abide in the truth," antichrists—especially junior ones—will never have a chance to lead them astray. But what does it mean to abide? Is it a state of perfection or a means to achieving such a state? Or is it something else completely? For the answers we will have to look at our next chapter.

## *Test Your Faith*

It is possible for some believers to see the information covered in this chapter as "old hat" and "stuff they already believe and don't have to worry about."

Use the following test to measure the importance of the incarnation in your thinking and actions.

1. The Deity of Christ is something:

      __a. I take for granted

      __b. I wish I knew more about

      __c. I value above all my other beliefs.

2. The anointing of the Holy Spirit is something:

      __a. I'm not sure I have

      __b. I hope I have

      __c. I know I have.

3. The danger of my being brainwashed by a cult or offbeat teacher is:

    \_\_a. Substantial

    \_\_b. Possible

    \_\_c. Slight.

4. When Jehovah's Witnesses come to call, I:

    \_\_a. Appear not to be home or just shut the door

    \_\_b. Try to talk to them but feel frustrated or inadequate

    \_\_c. Welcome the chance to witness to them in love.

5. In this chapter, Dorothy Sayers is quoted as saying that unless we believe rightly, there is not the faintest reason why we should believe at all. Do you:

    \_\_a. Disagree strongly

    \_\_b. Disagree somewhat

    \_\_c. Agree somewhat

    \_\_d. Agree strongly.

On a separate sheet of paper, write a brief paragraph giving reasons for your answer.

6. I am most tempted to quench the Holy Spirit by:

    \_\_a. Neglect of Bible reading and prayer

    \_\_b. Neglect of fellowship with other believers

    \_\_c. Going through all the right motions, but not changing very much.

---

### Notes

1. Dorothy Sayers, *The Emperor Constantine: A Chronical* (London: Victor Gollancz, 1951), p. 108.

2. 1 John 2:23, *The Living Bible*.

3. When Paul referred to the antichrist, he called him the "man of lawlessness"

who would oppose and exalt himself over God, even proclaiming his own deity while working all kinds of counterfeit miracles, signs and wonders (see 2 Thess. 2:1-12).

4. Scholars differ widely on what John meant in verse 18 by "the last hour." Three interpretations are widely held: (1) the last hour meant just that—those days just before the end of the world; (2) the last hour referred to the total Christian age, the time between Christ's first coming and His second; (3) the last hour was a "time of crisis" which John felt he and all other Christians were experiencing. Curtis Vaughn had problems with all three interpretations. For example, if interpretation (1) is completely correct it "seems a bit unlikely that the beloved disciple would claim knowledge which was admittedly denied to his Lord" (see Mark 13:32). After discussing flaws in interpretations (2) and (3), Vaughn concludes that he is "inclined to adopt, with slight modification, the first interpretation and to conclude that 'the last hour' has been prolonged far beyond what John would have imagined." See Curtis Vaughn, *1, 2, 3 John* (Grand Rapids: Zondervan Publishing House, 1970), pp. 60-62.

5. John may also have been familiar with Paul's final warning to the Ephesian elders at Miletus: "I know that after I leave, savage wolves will come in among you and will not spare the flock. Even from your own number men will arise and distort the truth in order to draw away disciples after them" (Acts 20:29,30).

6. For a good discussion of the meaning of anointing in 1 John 2:20, see Herschel H. Hobbs, *The Epistles of John* (Nashville: Thomas Nelson Inc., 1983), pp. 65, 66.

7. W. E. Vine, *The Epistles of John* (Grand Rapids: Zondervan Publishing House, 1970), p. 37.

8. William Barclay, *The Letters of John and Jude* Daily Study Bible (Edinburgh: The St. Andrew Press, 1958), p. 76.

9. Ibid., p. 79.

10. James Bjornstad, *Counterfeits at Your Door* (Ventura, CA: Regal Books, 1979), see especially Sections I and II, pp. 16-97.

11. Ibid., pp. 65-68. Bjornstad documents all his assertions to what Jehovah's Witnesses teach with references to their own literature. His book contains an extensive bibliography of Jehovah's Witness resources.

12. Ibid., p. 66.

13. Dorothy L. Sayers, *Creed or Chaos* (New York: Harcourt Brace Jovanovich Inc., 1949), p. 32.

14. Roy Laurin, *Life at Its Best* (Chicago: Van Kampen Press, 1946), p. 143.

15. John White, *The Race* (Downers Grove, IL: Inter-Varsity Press, 1984), p. 59.

16. John Stott, *The Epistles of John* (Grand Rapids: Wm. B. Eerdmans Publishing Co., 1960), p. 115.

# 8
# Blessed Assurance for Imperfect Christians

*Throw open the windows of my house*
*That Your salt breeze*
*May sweep through my stale habits*
*Blow over the fences*
*Of my self-pity*
*That I may run a race*
*Against my low opinion of myself*
*And win.*[1]
—*Robert Raines*

*Now we are children of God, and what we*
*will be has not yet been made known. But*
*we know that when he appears, we shall be*
*like him, for we shall see him as he is.*[2]
—*The Apostle John*

E arly in his ministry, Calvin Miller grew discouraged and impatient because so many in his congregation remained "very unlike Jesus." Was it his sermons or their apathy?

Particularly bothersome to Miller was a close friend who often invited him to lunch to talk about the Lord. But when the check came, Tom was in the restroom or looking the other way. It was a small thing but like the proverbial pebble in the shoe, it rankled. Miller prayed that God would show Tom "the rich testimony to Christ in paying his own way." But Tom seemed as oblivious to any urgings from God as he was to the check. Miller's heart "began to grow as closed toward him as his wallet was toward me."

Things got better only when Miller realized Tom wasn't the real problem, he was. He couldn't change Tom's stinginess, but he could do something about moving closer to Christ himself. Miller realized he was indulging in self-righteousness, spotting splinters in the eyes of his fellow Christians but unaware of logs in his own. As he came again and again to what he calls "the table of inwardness," Miller was humbled by how much Christ loved and accepted him in his own unfinished state. He began to see "how frequently I had drawn from the riches of Christ and repaid Him with a stingy obedience. Tom still isn't very generous, but at least I can pay with greater cheer . . . I have learned he and I are both unfinished."[3]

### Christians are "not yet beings"

Miller's candid admission reminds us that all Christians are unfinished, or are what he calls "not yet beings."[4] John would have liked the term. Nearing the age of 100, 70 or 80 years of which he had spent as a believer, John understood the Christian's "not yet" problem completely. That's why his letter is a blend of warnings and admonitions mixed with comfort and assurance. He has just finished one complete round of his three tests of the Christian. In 1 John 1:5–2:2, he gave his moral test—"Do I obey?" In 2:3-11, he gave the social test—"Do I love?" In 2:18-27, he gave a doctrinal test—"Do I believe?"

Now he will start his second round of tests, with a slight change of tone. He will still "sound the battle cry" as he afflicts the Gnostic heretics, but there will be a bit more "blessed assurance" as he comforts and encourages the Christian faithful whom the false teachers have been plaguing with feelings of inadequacy, uncertainty, confusion and failure. And so, continuing with his strong urging to stay close to Christ, John says:

### 1 John 2:28–3:3

And now, dear children, continue in him, so that when he appears we may be confident and unashamed before him at his coming.

If you know that he is righteous, you know that everyone who does what is right has been born of him.

How great is the love the Father has lavished on us, that we should be called children of God! And that is what we are! The reason the world does not know us is that it did not know him. Dear friends, now we are children of God, and what we will be has not yet been made known. But we know that when he appears, we shall be like him, for we shall see him as he is. Everyone who has this hope in him purifies himself, just as he is pure.

With John's flowing style, changes in emphasis and direction aren't always that evident. Verse 28 of chapter 2 is a gentle transition to what will be new ground. John started by comparing light and darkness. From here on he will not mention "the light" again, but will emphasize doing what is right by putting love into action.

John knows there are all kinds of systems and formulas for doing what is right, and they all depend on one thing: *abiding in*

*Christ* (see v. 28, *NASB*). The Greek word here is *meno*, which can also be translated "continue" *(NIV)* or "remain permanently" *(The Amplified Bible)*. It all comes down to staying close to Christ in order to be confident and unashamed when He returns.

John is most certainly referring to the *parousia*—Christ's Second Coming. John knows that every believer will face Christ with one of two basic attitudes: (1) confidence that comes from a life of trust and obedience, or (2) shame and fear because of failure to keep a good grip on the truth and continue walking steadily in the Light.

Obviously, many Christians have lived and died since John wrote these words, and Christ has not yet returned. John's concept still applies, however, because Christ still "appears" to the Christian when he or she leaves this earthly life. The old cliché asks, "Are you ready to meet your Maker?" The confident Christian answers, "Meet Him? I've been walking with Him everyday!"[5]

## What will it mean to be "like Him"?

In the first two verses of chapter 3, John gives Christians some of the most assuring words in the entire New Testament. Because Jesus is theirs, they are God's children and very special people! It's an honor to be a Christian, says John, but not something the world honors (see v. 1). Don't look to the world for your self-esteem cautions the old apostle. And most certainly, don't look to the Gnostic teachers who are trying to make you feel like inadequate, imperfect failures who "don't quite have it." John can just picture the false teachers in a strategy session saying things like, "What we have to do is soften up their self-esteem—then they'll fall like ripe plums into our theological basket."

Gnostic propaganda was rather basic and not all that subtle: "Do you have *real* spiritual knowledge?" they would ask. "Why all this childish concern about sins? Don't you know that the truly spiritual man is unaffected by a few 'sins'?"[6]

Notice that once again John equates the Gnostics with the world—the pagan secular system without God. John seldom sees a great deal of difference between the Gnostics and the world. The Gnostics tried to claim they had God, but they weren't even close. Gnostics thought they were spiritually complete, when in truth they hadn't even started.

Christians, on the other hand, were vulnerable to the confident but mistaken arguments of the Gnostics because any sincere believer recognizes he is still incomplete and has a long way to go. Christians feel the "not-yet-ness" of their lives because God's touch has made them sensitive to the dangers and power of sin. After Christ enters our lives, we look with new and different eyes upon what God has done—and is doing. That is why 1 John 3:2 is such good news. We are children of God and that's just the beginning. We're not even sure what we will become, but whatever happens, we're going to see Jesus as He really is, and become just like Him!

Have you ever thought about "being like *Him*"? What does that mean to you exactly? For some it might mean no more aches and pains, no more wheelchairs, iron lungs or insulin shots. Others might think of finally having enough to eat, a decent place to live, or soaring free from a Gulag concentration camp.

For many it will be "the end of the struggle" in one way or another. Anger, fear, lack of self-esteem, boredom, feelings of failure, frustrations, disappointments, deadlines, pressures, alarm clocks, freeways, diapers, potty training will all be gone when we look into His eyes and know exactly what He is like.

It is true, of course, that being children of God helps us in the struggle *now*. Sometimes we win mighty victories. At other times progress seems slow, and occasionally we feel we're getting nowhere—the "not-yet-ness" turns into "maybe never"! But whatever the case, being a Christian means that we are infinitely better than we were and the best is yet to come.

## We have to trust the process

Just how should a Christian respond to all this good news? Kick back and relax? Loosen up a bit and not be so straight and stodgy? The Gnostics (and their modern-day cousins) would like that. They love to expound on the idea that the truly spiritual man can sin and not be harmed. John can even hear the false teachers taking unsuspecting Christians aside and saying, "Let us make life a little easier. After all, nobody's perfect. Wouldn't you like to know how to be a Christian without having to toe the line *all* the time?"

John knows the answer to that one. He knows there is a delicate balance between being a Christian without being perfect and being imperfect but remaining genuinely Christian. The secret is in trusting God's process for completing our "not yet" lives.

For John, a sign that you are trusting God's process is that you are trying to stay pure—as pure as Jesus Himself (see v. 3). Staying *that* pure is serious business. In fact, it's impossible. At the other end of the spectrum from pure is corrupted—totally contaminated. What about the in-between where "not-yet-ones" struggle? How sinful can a Christian be and still retain the high hope of "being like Christ"? John sees it like this:

### 1 John 3:4-10

Everyone who sins breaks the law; in fact, sin is lawlessness. But you know that he appeared so that he might take away our sins. And in him is no sin. No one who lives in him keeps on sinning. No one who continues to sin has either seen him or known him.

Dear children, do not let anyone lead you astray. He who does what is right is righteous, just as he is righteous. He who does what is sinful is of the devil, because the devil has been sinning from the beginning. The reason the Son of God appeared was to destroy the devil's work. No one who is born of God will continue to sin, because God's seed remains in him; he cannot go on sinning, because he has been born of God. This is how we know who the children of God are and who the children of the devil are: Anyone who does not do what is right is not a child of God; neither is anyone who does not love his brother.

In these two paragraphs, John takes dead aim on the Gnostic's double standard concerning behavior. The Gnostics claimed to be the spiritually elite who knew the right secrets that put them above law or any moral code. They taught that the truly spiritual man could sin to his heart's content because his spirit and his body were separate. "What I do with my body has nothing to do with my spirit," said the Gnostic sophisticates. John's answer is, "Nonsense—show me how you treat your body and that will tell me the exact condition of your spirit."

### Does a "real Christian" never sin?

In verses 4 to 6, John makes it clear that anyone who wants to call himself "Christian" is concerned about his morals—obeying the law. Christians are redeemed and no longer depend on keeping the law for salvation, but that does not mean they disregard the law. John would agree completely with Paul who argued in his letter to the Romans, "What shall we say, then? Shall we go on sinning so that grace may increase? By no means!" (Rom. 6:1,2). In a word, says John, "sin is lawlessness" (1 John 3:4). Breaking the law doesn't make a person a sinner; people break the law because at the very base they are sinners. The difference is vast.

Because people are sinners, Christ came to take away their sins (see v. 5). There is no sin in Christ and anyone who chooses to live in Christ does not sin. In fact, says John, anyone who sins doesn't really know Christ at all! (See v. 6.)

For believers who are acutely aware of their incomplete "not yet" state, verse 6 doesn't sound like very good news. Didn't John clearly say earlier in his letter that anyone who denies being a sinner is a liar (see 1 John 1:8,10)? And didn't he also clearly say that if anyone sins, Jesus Christ will be his advocate (see 1 John 2:1)? And why did John give us 1 John 1:9 if it wasn't his clear intention to help us know how to find cleansing and forgiveness when we do sin?

There are all kinds of theories on what John means in verse 5 of this third chapter.[7] For example:

*One.* Real Christians do not sin, period. (This

view is held by perfectionists, as well as people who spend a great deal of time with psychiatrists.)

*Two*. Real Christians might commit minor sins, but nothing major like murder. (This "limited sin" concept has similarities to the Roman Catholic concept of mortal versus venial sins.)

*Three*. Real Christians don't sin because God has a different standard for them than He has for unbelievers. (This sounds suspiciously like the Gnostics and their secret knowledge that put them "beyond sin.")

*Four*. Real Christians don't sin in their "new nature" although their old nature might slip up from time to time. (Another way of looking at it is to say the "born-again" spirit in man cannot sin, but the body still does.)

*Five*. Real Christians sin in reality but have an ideal goal or standard not to sin. (This idea has some merit and fits in with the unlimited potential John claims for all God's children back in 3:1,2).

*Six*. The real Christian does not commit habitual, consistent sin as he did before salvation. Knowing Christ doesn't make him perfect, but there is a definite difference.

This last view has the most going for it for several reasons:

• John is hardly an ivory tower idealist. It is because he knows the facts of life that he is writing his Epistle in the first place. John is well aware that all Christians sin and constantly need forgiveness. Whatever he means by "Christians do not sin" he is not suggesting that Christians are perfect or sinless.

• Translating the Greek language is difficult and in some places what translators put down is not as clear as it could be. That is the case with 1 John 3:6.

• In John's letter the tenses of his Greek verbs are critical. Back in 1 John 2:1 he told his readers that he was writing "so that you will not sin." In 2:1 the verb "sin" is in what scholars call the *aorist tense*—which always indicates a particular and definite act. So, in 2:1, John is talking about particular and individual acts of sin which Christians must resist the temptation to commit. If they do happen to commit these acts of sin, John says they have an advocate with the Father in Jesus Christ, who will plead their case and gain their forgiveness (see 1 John 2:1,2).

• In 1 John 3:6 the verb used for "to sin" is in the *present tense*. In verse 6, John is not talking about individual acts of sin. He is referring to "continuous, constant and habitual action." In other words, anyone who walks with Christ and "abides with Him" will not make sin an habitual way of life. The Christian may yield to temptation and commit individual acts of sin, but he or she will never live continually with sin as a welcome and valued part of his or her life-style.

## Trust God and sin bravely?

The last thing John is trying to do in this passage is set up some kind of impossible standard of sinless perfectionism for all Christians. All Christians are bound to commit sins. That's why Martin Luther told believers of his generation to "trust God and sin on bravely." Was Luther a Gnostic in disguise? Hardly. When he advised Christians to "sin on bravely" he was being a realist. As long as Christians trust God and Christ's atonement, they know their mistakes are covered. But Martin Luther would have been the first to join in saying that a Christian *never* sins carelessly and continuously as he did before he came to Christ.

We don't need three guesses to know who John is talking about in verse 7. He could just as well have written, "Dear children, don't let the Gnostics lead you astray." The Christian does what is right as he seeks to follow Christ. To live fast and loose as the Gnostics did is to follow the devil. The Gnostics weren't saved. They were lost, doing what the devil has done from the very beginning. The devil had the entire world in his grip until the Son of God appeared. God lived among us in the form of Jesus Christ to save us from our sins, "undoing the devil's work" (v. 8, *Phillips*).

In verses 9 and 10, John nails down his argument by repeating the same idea he introduced in verse 6: Christians don't keep on sinning because they have God's seed within them. As Peter put it, we are "born again, not of perishable seed but of imperishable, through the living and enduring word of God" (1 Pet. 1:23). Those with the real seed growing within are children of God. Those without it are children of the devil. The devil's children don't do what is right. In fact, they aren't even interested (see 1 John 3:10).

For John it's all quite simple. If you are a child of God you will do what is right—or at least be very interested in trying to do so—because you love God and know that He has forgiven you and wants you to live a righteous life. But if sin does not bother you, and you seem to be able to commit any number of questionable acts with no particular pangs of conscience, John is quite firm in saying you really aren't in God's family and you never were.[8]

### Sin is a problem, not a defeat

As usual John mixes assurance and encouragement with challenge and responsibility. On the assuring and encouraging side, John is telling Christians, "Look, I'm not saying Christians have to be perfect. God doesn't demand a life that is sinless, but He does demand that we be ever on guard against sin. He wants us to never surrender as we fight the battle for goodness. We must always see sin as a temporary problem or error but never a permanent state of defeat."[9]

John's words are also encouraging to believers when they face those situations that could be labeled, "I'll sin if I do and I'll sin if I don't." Robert Raines pictures that kind of dilemma perfectly as he prays:

> I have to decide Yes or No
> and neither option seems wholly right
> but there is no third possibility

not to decide is to decide
so I must decide one way
or the other . . .
either way
somebody gets hurt
there's no painless, pure way through
my hands are tied
there are limits and I've reached them
how can I justify what I have to do?
to the parties involved?
to myself?
to you?

. . . . . . . . . . . . . . . . . .
Lord, will you go with me
as I decide?
cover my inevitable sin with your grace
accept me
even when I'm unacceptable
let my Yes or No
be born out of
a brave trust[10]

Along with his assurance and encouragement we hear John giving us a challenge to be responsible and mature. Christians have unlimited potential and they shouldn't waste it (see 1 John 3:1,2). We are never to take sin lightly, to become content with our pet sinful patterns and indulge ourselves on the grounds that, "Well, no one's perfect, and besides God understands." There is a type of Gnostic thinking that is still alive and on the loose in the Church today. It can be found in all sorts of shapes and sizes, some of which sound quite innocent and even spiritual:

- "God is my friend."
- "God is my care giver."
- "God understands."
- "God never puts me on a guilt trip."
- "I'm under grace, not Law."

Every one of the above phrases is true, but only half true. Emphasize the wrong half and you are in danger of indulging yourself in what Dietrich Bonhoeffer called "cheap grace."

It is true that God is our Friend who cares and understands, but He is also our sovereign Lord (see Rom. 9:19-21).

It is true that God never puts people on guilt trips; they manage to do that quite nicely themselves. The Lord is, however, the source of "godly sorrow" which "brings repentance that leads to salvation" (2 Cor. 7:10).

It is true that those in Christ Jesus are under grace, not the condemnation of the Law, but they are also obligated to let the Holy Spirit work in their lives in such a way that the righteous requirements to the Law are fully met (see Rom. 8:1-4).

## We are imperfect, but in God's process

Often accused of being a black-and-white thinker, John is showing us the delicate balance in the Christian life. To see that balance clearly, we need to circle back to verses 1 and 2 of chapter 3 of 1 John. We are "not yet" beings. We are incomplete and capable of more sin than we care to admit. Nonetheless, we are God's beloved children and that's just the beginning. We can't imagine how wonderful it's going to be farther down the line. Meanwhile, we are to stay pure—as pure as Christ Himself (see v. 3).

John doesn't spell out what "staying pure" involves, but everything he says in verses 4 through 10 suggests that staying pure is more a matter of dealing with the inside, not the outside.

We can reform the outside quite easily: go to church, use the right spiritual jargon, learn to pray aloud eloquently, etc. But on the inside lie the frontiers of real purification and change: being loving, fair and patient; spending quality time in the Scriptures and struggling at the toughest work of all—prayer. It's one thing to make a beginning at doing all this; it's another to stay with it. New beginnings are much easier than the long follow-through.[11]

You can almost see the twinkle in John's eyes when he assumes that we're game for that long follow-through. Because we're Christians, *naturally* we will want to do what is righteous. We will want to live pure lives and not practice continual sin.

Once again we find ourselves clearing our throats, straightening our ties, smoothing our skirts and saying, "Of course, John, you're absolutely right, but could you excuse me for a moment? I have a little thinking—and growing—to do!"

## Test Your Faith

Perfectionism—the attitude that says "I never do as well as I should and God must not be pleased"—is a disease that afflicts many Christians. The cure to perfectionism is to see yourself in God's process, not yet perfect but allowing Him to develop and mature your potential.

Below are two columns. On the left are descriptions and remarks that fit perfectionists. On the right are descriptions and remarks that would be more typical of Christians who realize they are not perfect but in God's process. Read each item carefully and decide where you fit:

| | | |
|---|---|---|
| You can set goals that are always out of reach | OR | You can strive for excellence within your capabilities. |
| —"I have to keep raising my sights—God wants me to have goals that honor Him!" | | —"Show me Lord, what you want me to do. Give me your strength to do it." |
| You can think that you only count when you perform | OR | You can put your emphasis on being what God wants. |
| —"Talk is cheap. It's what I *do* for God that counts!" | | —"Help me, Lord, be the kind of person you want me to be." |

Tough sledding can get you down and depressed OR Disappointments can drive you closer to Christ.

___ "What's the use? The harder I try to live right, the more I foul it up."

___ "Lord, things aren't going all that well. Keep me going straight ahead—following you."

Failure can wipe you out OR Failure can be a step toward growth.

___ "How could I be *so stupid?* I don't deserve to be called a Christian!"

___ "Forgive me, Lord, for failing again. I'm trusting you to change me."

You can dwell on mistakes OR Learn from them.

___ "Forgetting to tell the rest of the committee about the change in the meeting time was really poor. I only did it once all year but it really bothers me."

___ "Lord, you know I tend to forget things. Help me keep my 'to do' list current!"

You can always "have to be Number One" OR You can try your best and leave the rest to God.

___ "Christians are too satisfied with mediocrity. If I do something, I want it to be first class!"

___ "Lord, I want to give it all I've got—but I've only got as much as I'm willing to let you give me."

You can hate criticism of    OR    You can accept criticism
any kind                            and profit from it.

—"How could they be so             —"Thanks, Lord, I needed
unappreciative after all            that word from John and
the work I do around                the others. They have a
here!"                              good point."

Winning can be the only      OR    Playing the game well is
thing                               what really counts.

—"Losers finish second. I          —"Lord, you know I like
can't stand being a loser.          to win, but no matter
I don't think God can               where I finish, your love
stand losers either."               makes me a winner."[12]

---

**Notes**

1. Robert Raines, *Lord, Could You Make It a Little Better?* (Waco: Word, Inc., 1972), p. 39.
2. 1 John 3:2.
3. Calvin Miller, *The Table of Inwardness* (Downers Grove, IL: Inter-Varsity Press, 1984), p. 59.
4. Ibid., pp. 57,58.
5. William Barclay, *The Letters of John and Jude* The Daily Study Bible (Edinburgh: The St. Andrew Press, 1958), p. 84.
6. Earl Palmer, *The Communicator's Commentary, 1, 2, 3 John, Revelation* (Waco: Word, Inc., 1982), p.53.
7. All twelve views are discussed thoroughly (if not exhaustively) by Robert L. Thomas, professor of Theology, Talbot Theological Seminary, in his syllabus entitled "Exegetical Digest of 1 John." Dr. Thomas's personal position incorporates the concept that the Christian does not commit habitual and consistent sin, that is, sin does not characterize his life, but adds the important distinction that for the Christian "there is not an unbroken continuity of sin from the past into the present, with that continuing present characteristic in the life of the one abiding in Christ. In terms of this approach, 3:9 means, 'it cannot be said of anyone who has been begotten of God that he has been doing sin and continues to do so in the present.' As for 3:9, the meaning is 'It cannot be said of the one begotten of God that he is able to have sinned in the past, continuing into the present, with sin

still characteristic of his life.' . . . What is John saying then? He is saying that an unbroken state of sinful behavior from the past into the present and continuing in the present, such as characterizes the children of the devil (cf. 3:10), is impossible for the one who has been begotten by God. He is describing a continuous condition such as characterizes the devil, and saying that anyone who experiences that same condition has not seen Christ or known him (cf. 3:6)." Robert L. Thomas, "Exegetical Digest of 1 John," Talbot Seminary, p. 260.

8. John Stott, *The Epistles of John* (Grand Rapids: Wm. B. Eerdmans Publishing Co., 1960), p. 126.

9. Barclay, *The Letters of John* pp. 96-97.

10. Raines, *Lord, Could You Make It a Little Better?*, p. 65.

11. Eugene Peterson, *Run With the Horses* (Downers Grove, IL: Inter-Varsity Press, 1983), p. 67.

12. Adapted from Kevin Leman, *The Birth Order Book* (Old Tappan, NJ: Fleming H. Revell, Co., 1984), p. 70.

# 9

# Prescription for a Clear Christian Conscience

*O Divine Master,
grant that I may not so much seek
to be consoled, as to console;
to be understood, as to understand;
to be loved, as to love;
for it is in giving that we receive,
it is in pardoning that we are
pardoned,
and it is in dying that we are born
to eternal life.*[1]
—*Saint Francis of Assisi*

*Little children, let us stop just* saying *we
love people; let us* really *love them, and
show it* by our actions.[2]
—*The Apostle John*

We are just about halfway through the 105 verses in the Epistle of 1 John. Because of all the Gnostic mischief, John has been spending a lot of time describing what you might call a "real Christian." Actually, John would simply say "Christian." By definition, you can't be a false Christian—either you are a Christian or you are not.

John's definition of a real Christian is based on his three tests to expose Gnostic lies and heresies. In the last passage (1 John 2:28–3:10), the apostle covered a second version of his "moral test." According to John, a Christian (not a Gnostic counterfeit) is, or does, the following:

- Has a confidence that comes from living closely to Christ (abiding with Him) and seeking to do what is right (see 2:28,29)
- Rejoices in being a child of God who has untapped potential for becoming (see 3:2)
- Seeks to be pure as Christ is pure (see 3:3)
- Above all, has nothing to do with willfully, deliberately and habitually committing acts of sin (see 3:4-10).

If John were having a conversation with some believers he might put it this way: "You want to know if you're among the sheep or the goats? Check your attitude toward sin. If God's seed—His living Word—has taken root in your life, you won't make sin a continual habit. I'm not saying that you will be sinless. The Gnostics make that impossible claim by saying they have special knowledge that puts them beyond sin, but that's foolish talk. Anyone is bound to sin at times. Any believer can fall into sin but no Christian will walk in sin—or wallow in it."[3]

Because the Gnostics were such an insidious threat, John has had to spend a lot of time accentuating the negative. But now he will shift his emphasis from moral to social, from "don'ts" to "do's." According to the old apostle, Christians do not habitually and continuously sin. They *do* stay busy reaching out in love—especially to one another. The Gnostics who had infiltrated the church fellowship were doing the exact opposite and that's why John goes on to say:

### 1 John 3:11-15

This is the message you heard from the beginning: We should love one another. Do not be like Cain, who belonged to the evil one and murdered his brother. And why did he murder him? Because his own actions were evil and his brother's were righteous. Do not be surprised, my brothers, if the world hates you. We know that we have passed from death to life, because we love our brothers. Anyone who does not love remains in death. Anyone who hates his brother is a murderer, and you know that no murderer has eternal life in him.

Back in chapter 2 of his letter (vv. 7-11), John sketched in his first social test for Christians by referring to the "new/old command" they have had from the beginning—to love one another (see 2:7). Here in chapter 3 he refers again to the message Christians have heard from the beginning—"love one another" (v. 11). In his typical black-and-white style, John minces no words. If you love your brothers, it proves you have eternal life. If you hate them, it proves you are still dead in your sins (see v. 14).

The Gnostics thought that it was perfectly acceptable for the spiritually enlightened man to look down on those who "weren't in his class." They had such disdain for the person who could not claim special esoteric knowledge like theirs that their attitude could easily be described as hatred. In searching for a good example to contrast this kind of behavior with the kind of love the Christian should show, John goes back to Cain, the first recorded murderer in history. Scripture does not explain why Cain slew Abel, but jealousy had to be part of the problem. Evidently God found Cain's actions evil and Abel's righteous. Cain's hatred literally drove him to butcher his brother.[4]

## The legacy of Boris Kornfeld

John sees Cain as a prototype of the world that hated Christ and continues to hate any Christian whose clear and visible testimony makes it uncomfortable. In his gripping book *Loving God*, Charles Colson shares the story of Boris Kornfeld, a Russian medical doctor who was sentenced to a Communist slave labor camp for an unnamed political crime. Kornfeld's background was Jewish, but he had not been serious about his religion for years.

In prison, Kornfeld met a devout Christian who led him to Christ. Things are bad enough for anyone in a Russian labor camp, but for a former Jew now become Christian things can get bad indeed. The doctor started to stand up for what was right and began reporting thievery of food from patients by hospital orderlies. He also refused to remain silent while guards brutalized and neglected prisoners, who died as a result.

Kornfeld became a marked man and began sleeping in the prison hospital office because he knew to sleep in the barracks would mean certain death. Paradoxically, however, he became bolder in his stand for justice. As Chuck Colson observes, "Having accepted the possibility of death, Boris Kornfeld was now free to live."[5]

But Kornfeld also longed to tell someone about his newfound faith. One afternoon, as he examined a young man who had just been operated on for stomach cancer, Kornfeld began to share his testimony. Throughout the afternoon and into the night, he told of his discovery of Christ, as his patient drifted back and forth between a feverish sleep and painful wakefulness. The young man couldn't quite believe what Kornfeld was saying but he was entranced by the doctor's passionate words.

Finally, the young cancer patient fell asleep for the night and didn't awaken until the next morning when a fellow patient whispered that Dr. Kornfeld had been attacked and killed during the night. Cain had struck again in the form of a plasterer's mallet wielded with murderous intent. Had the world really won? The young man to whom Kornfeld had witnessed went on to become a Christian, survived prison camp and lived to tell about it with a pen that shook the world. His name? Alexander Solzhenitsyn.[6]

Boris Kornfeld's story is a stark example of how the world can hate the Christian who becomes "bothersome." John remembered well the words Jesus spoke at the Last Supper. If the Christian belonged to the world, the world would love him dearly. But the Christian is chosen *out* of the world by the one the world first hated—Jesus Christ. And those chosen by Christ are the ones the world will hate (see John 15:18,19).[7]

But Boris Kornfeld's sacrifice is also a challenging and triumphant description of the kind of love John is talking about—love that *does* something for others:

### 1 John 3:16-24

This is how we know what love is: Jesus Christ laid down his life for us. And we ought to lay down our lives for our brothers. If anyone has material possessions and sees his brother in need but has no pity on him, how can the love of God be in him? Dear children, let us not love with words or tongue but with actions and in truth. This then is how we know that we belong to the truth, and how we set our hearts at rest in his presence whenever our hearts condemn us. For God is greater than our hearts, and he knows everything.

Dear friends, if our hearts do not condemn us, we have confidence before God and receive from him anything we ask, because we obey his commands and do what pleases him. And this is his command: to believe in the name of his Son, Jesus Christ, and to love one another as he commanded us. Those who obey his commands live in him, and he in them. And this is how we know that he lives in us: We know it by the Spirit he gave us.

Do you want to know what love is? John says you need look

no further than the Cross where Christ laid down His life for us. Do you want to know how to love others? Lay down your life for them!

Stories of people who lay down their lives for others are almost always impressive because, for most of us, the idea of making that kind of total sacrifice is only that—an idea. One of the most poignant tales of such sacrifice is the one involving twin brothers, one of whom was dying of kidney failure. The only hope for the sick boy was a kidney transplant from his healthy twin.

When asked if he would donate a kidney to save his brother's life, the youngster swallowed hard and agreed to do it. Just before the operation the doctors found him weeping as he was being prepared for surgery. Why? He was quite sure that if he donated a kidney he would die and, while he was willing to die for his brother, he was understandably not too overjoyed by the prospect![8]

## How do you love God?

But what do we do if we can't "lay down our lives" for someone? Opportunities for this kind of sacrifice don't come along everyday and, frankly, if we are honest we will admit that we're glad they don't. John has the answer. You don't have to die on a cross, on a battlefield or on an operating table for your brother. Just give him what he needs out of your own abundance, or even your own inadequate resources. In other words, quit simply *talking* about love and actually *do* something loving (see vv. 17,18). One way to define this action-oriented love might be this:

> Love is willingly giving up
> something that I enjoy, want or
> need in order to bless, help, or
> positively affect someone else.

But there is still more to love than that. Christ came to seek and save those who had the most desperate need of all (see Luke 19:10). His followers are to seek out those who need a helping hand, a loving word or touch.

One reason Chuck Colson wrote *Loving God* was that he did an informal survey among friends and acquaintances and asked: "How do you love God?" He heard all kinds of stammering answers, none too specific nor revealing. Two that ranked highest on the list were: attending church and tithing! And so Colson went out to gather stories, illustrations and ideas that would explain what it means to "love God."

He found that loving God is being a U.S. senator who takes time to read the Bible to a friend dying of cancer; loving God is being a businessman who buys a multi-million dollar motel and gives up thousands of dollars each month because he chooses not to serve liquor; loving God is being a secretary who gives up her lunch hours and eats peanut butter sandwiches while she drives to and from the county correctional institution where she spends every noon with inmates, talking, studying the Bible— whatever they need.[9]

## The most valuable thing we can ever give
Most translations of 1 John 3:17 suggest that Christians can lay down their lives for others by giving tangible things like "material possessions"(*NIV*), "money" (*TLB*), and "the world's goods" (*NASB*). The Greek word here is *bios,* which means life or that which is essential to living. It is the same word used in Mark 12:44 when Jesus speaks of the widow who gave two mites and *"cast in all that she had, even all her living"* (*KJV*).

To be sure, there are many instances in which the proper loving response is to send a check or bring over a box of clothes or food. Notice, however, in two of the three illustrations above, the Christian involved gave time more than anything else. The senator could give the dying cancer victim no real help except his own presence at the patient's bedside, spending last precious minutes with him. The secretary couldn't buy the prison inmates their freedom, but she gave them her lunch hours.

If *bios* is that which is essential to living, surely time is included. In fact, many of us would have to say that there is little in life more precious than our time. It is easy to say, "I'll call you next week," or "I'm definitely going to drop by soon." It is quite another thing to do it. Somehow the seconds melt into minutes and the minutes into hours, and the hours into days that are gone faster than last week's paycheck.

How do we love God and others? John's answer is that we examine how we really live: what we do, what we say, where we go and *how we spend what is really valuable to us.*

## The best way to handle doubts and guilt trips

John goes on to say that loving God by loving others has a payoff. He isn't talking about checks miraculously arriving in the mail, or coming home after being fired, only to have the phone ring with a job that's twice as good as your old one. And he certainly isn't talking about warm fuzzy feelings of spiritual superiority; he'll leave that for the Gnostics who were masters of the art.

Remember that John is writing to reassure Christians who are confused and even discouraged. Some of them are probably ready to "bag the whole thing" because they can't measure up to the impossible standards of perfection they keep hearing about from these new enlightened teachers who keep stopping by to hold a Bible study. The Gnostics had the Christians so twisted around that they weren't sure what the truth was or if they had very much of it.

In verse 19, John says that any Christian can know if he or she belongs to the truth. Just check your own life—what have you been doing to love others? The old cliché, "Actions speak louder than words" has a double meaning here.

When you think about it, a lot of the Christian life is talk. We talk doctrine; we proclaim our faith in God and His only Son Jesus Christ our Lord conceived by the Holy Ghost, born of the Virgin Mary, suffering under Pontius Pilate, crucified and risen from the dead the third day . . . ; we vow that sin will never dominate our thinking or become a habit in our lives. But no matter how fervently we voice our commitments, we have those moments of failure, followed by frustration, doubt and fear.

These are the times when our hearts condemn us, but John assures us that even in these dark moments our hearts can be at rest, because "God is *greater than our hearts*" (read vv. 19 and 20 as one sentence). What does John mean by this?

Many commentators speculate that John is taking a brief time out from his basic game plan, which is to run his second series of tests of the Christian. He began chapter 3 of his letter with the moral test, and in the passage we are studying here he moved into his social test. But he seems to sense that there are many believers who are more sensitive, perfectionistic, introspective or melancholy than others. Verses 19 through 24 of chapter 3 are especially for them.

To understand what John is talking about in verses 19 and 20, it helps to substitute "conscience" for "heart" (see *NEB* translation). We all know what it's like to have the conscience condemn us. The conscience is a God-given faculty to help us tell right from wrong, but it is not infallible. Your conscience can put you on a guilt trip—that is, make you wallow in false guilt because you think you haven't done enough, you've failed God, you're a "lousy Christian," etc.

Some people believe the Holy Spirit is the conscience, but this is not so. The Holy Spirit works in your life, teaching you what is true. In fact, the Holy Spirit is the One who helps reassure your heart just in case your conscience starts working overtime to condemn you when, in truth, you don't deserve that much condemnation.

The Holy Spirit is the One who truly knows your heart. He knows your real motives and deepest resolves. We may have the best of intentions, but there are always situations where we fail and do things that some people (including ourselves) find "unforgivable." Daily life is filled with land mines of all shapes and sizes. When these situations explode, we wind up writhing on the spit of conscience:

- An exhausted mother of three preschoolers finds her three-year-old accidentally making a mess that will take at least 30 minutes to clean up and she lashes out with a severe spanking. Later, when she cools off, she realizes the child was only trying to help.
- A man asks his friend at work an innocent question while others are listening at coffee break, and to his horror he later learns he has "let the cat out of the

bag" and ruined that friend's chances for promotion.
- A husband tries to help with the dishes and breaks an antique dish his wife has treasured for years.
- A wife forgets to tell her husband as he leaves for work their car is low on gas. Before he notices it, he runs out, with the nearest station more than two miles away. By the time he gets gas, he's missed an important appointment.
- The wedding shower hostess depends on you to bring the prizes for the games. You forget and this makes the hostess look disorganized. She lets you know she was "terribly embarrassed."

Everyone faces sticky situations. Sometimes we bring them on ourselves; in other cases they simply happen. Either way they can cause unpleasant guilt trips. It's all too common to tell ourselves: "I'm a Christian. I should have been more sensitive, more careful. I, above all people, should have known better!"

John's answer to this kind of breast-beating is in verse 20 of chapter 3. When our conscience puts us on trial, so to speak, God is our court of first and last resort. He is "greater than our conscience" because He *knows all*. He knows—when we can't be sure—if we have been loving or if we at least *meant* to be loving!

One good test of how sincerely we mean to be loving is our sense of responsibility. Does the buck stop with us or do we like to pass it on?

### When the buck stopped with Bill Lear

Bill Lear, inventor of the Learjet, an eight-seat, 560 MPH, aircraft designed especially for fast economical travel by business executives, had the buck stop on his desk in 1966. The first Learjet had come off the assembly lines in 1963 and 55 were in the air with another 15 on order. But in one month, two Learjets mysteriously crashed, both with fatalities.

No on could explain the crashes, which happened shortly after takeoff. Was it pilot error—or a flaw in the plane's design? Bill Lear didn't know, but he decided to ground all the planes until he could find out.

"Don't do it!" his executives chorused. "We're under no legal obligation—the public will lose confidence in all Learjets. It will ruin all of us!"

Lear thought that over. His execs were right. Admitting possible fault when there was a good chance there wasn't any was bad business. At the same time, what about his responsibility? What if another Learjet crashed before he could find the problem—if there was actually a problem to find?

Bill Lear sat alone one night in the cockpit of his personal Learjet, thinking it all through. He remembered his boyhood and the enumerable sermons his paster had preached on honesty and having the courage to do what is right—what God expects. Before he left that cockpit, Lear made his decision.

Learjet owners across the world were contacted and advised to ground their planes until further notice. The papers got wind of the story. It made headlines and soon contracts for new planes were cancelled. But Bill Lear stuck with his decision. He took his own plane apart, piece by piece. He tried every lead, but nothing seemed to make sense.

As Lear went back over the details of both crashes, a simple pattern took shape: a takeoff in a rainstorm, a climb to 24,000 feet, a leveling off and then disappearance on the radar screen. Lear reexamined the entire plane and when he came to the tail assembly he noted the drain holes in the elevators which were designed to get rid of any water that might collect there. Could it be that both the ill-fated planes had climbed through the rainstorms, reached 24,000 feet (and much colder atmosphere) where the rainwater froze before it had a chance to completely drain away? What would happen when the pilot picked up speed with the extra weight of the ice in the tail elevators?

Lear had to find out. He fastened weights to each elevator that would equal that of frozen rainwater, took off and climbed to 24,000 feet where he leveled and poured on the fuel. As he hit 550 MPH, the plane seemed to go crazy and he was barely able to keep it under control. Somehow he reduced speed, leveled off and managed to land safely. A simple change in the drain hole design was all that was needed, and in three days teams of mechanics made the correction in Learjets across the world.

While the error was corrected in just a few days, it took more than a year for public confidence to return. When it did, sales of Learjets were better than ever. But Bill Lear hadn't risked his entire business and possibly his life just to increase sales. His sense of responsibility had kept him from passing the buck; his strong commitment to doing what is right—actually, to loving others—helped him make a tough decision when his heart (conscience) was sending more than a few condemning signals. He could have copped out and said, "Let them prove something is wrong with my beautiful plane." Or he could have gotten totally discouraged over the fact that two crashes had already killed people and he was to blame. But instead, he did what was right—what he knew God wanted him to do, because God was greater than the situation.

### False guilt vs. godly sorrow

In any situation, the key is to be able to tell the difference between copping out and trusting God who is greater than our hearts and knows us far better than we know ourselves. Obviously, there are times when we are at fault. If our hearts are not right we will feel pangs of guilt, but it will be the right kind of guilt. Scripture calls it "godly sorrow" which leads to real repentance, confession and reconciliation. The apostle Paul coins the term "godly sorrow" in verse 10 of 2 Corinthians 7 when he mentions the joy he feels as Titus brings him news from the Corinthian Church about their deep sorrow and concern for him after the rift that had been caused in the past.

If there was any church where things went wrong for Paul, it was in Corinth. His first letter to the Corinthians is more than proof of that. He had to rebuke them and point out where they were definitely wrong. But in his second letter he speaks of reconciliation. He is somewhere in Macedonia when Titus arrives with the news that the saints at Corinth have decided to act like saints and not carnal children. Paul's joy overflows and he says that even though he had to cause the Corinthians sorrow he does not regret it because it's the kind of sorrow that leads to real repentance (see 2 Cor. 7:8,9).

Godly sorrow equals true guilt—feeling to blame when you

definitely are. The important thing to note is that godly sorrow always brings repentance and a desire to change. Godly sorrow leads to salvation—setting things right, being saved and cleansed from sin. By contrast, worldly sorrow is always marked by pride, anger and selfish concern for oneself instead of concern for others. Worldly sorrow leads nowhere but to death. To put in another way, godly sorrow leads *to* God, worldly sorrow leads *aways from* God to destruction.

Many commentators feel that here in the third chapter of his letter John is trying to reassure Christians who feel the pain of being less than perfect in their walk with Christ. He wants to reassure committed Christians who still feel like failures a lot of the time. John's purpose is to heal the Christian's wounded conscience, not open the wound wider.[11]

In *The Living Bible* paraphrase, Ken Taylor puts an interesting interpretation on 1 John 3:20. "But if we have bad consciences and feel that we have done wrong, the Lord will surely feel it even more, for he knows everything we do." In the study edition of *The Living Bible,* Harold Lindsell comments in a footnote that "the Lord will surely feel it even more" could perhaps mean "the Lord will be merciful anyway." In the literal Greek the phrase reads, "If our heart condemns us, God is greater than our heart." What John could be saying is that either way, with true guilt or false, the Christian who sincerely seeks to love the brethren can find mercy by turning to the Lord. The keys are attitude and motivation.

## Benefits of a clear conscience

And what are the signs that we have the right attitude? John lists several:

First, we have the confidence to approach God in total trust, without fear. The Greek word for confidence (*parresia*) had a base meaning that dealt with freedom of speech—the valued right of a citizen to speak his mind.[12] As children in God's family, we have the right and privilege to speak our minds and come to God with whatever is on our hearts.

Second, we have the confidence that our prayers will be answered. The Christian whose heart does not condemn him has confidence to pray to God and know that he will receive anything he asks for. Why? Because he obeys God's commands and does what pleases Him (vv. 21, 22).

It all sounds fairly simple. Is God giving Christians *carte blanche* to "name it and claim it"? Hardly. The "commands" we are to obey is really one big commandment with two parts: (1) to believe in the name of the Son, and (2) to love one another as the Son commanded (see v. 23).

The result of our obedience is a blessing with two parts: (1) We abide (live) in Christ, and (2) He abides (lives) in us. John's *carte blanche* promise has a major qualifier: We must be living close enough to Christ to want what He wants—to know God's will for us and want to do it. John will repeat this concept with even more emphasis in chapter 5 when he will say, "If we ask anything according to his will, he hears us" (v. 14).

And how can we know we are in His will? How can we know that He lives in us? By the very same Spirit that he gave to each one of us at salvation. Indeed, we cannot love, we cannot believe, we cannot obey God without the Holy Spirit working within us. As John himself wrote in his Gospel, the Holy Spirit is the one who convicts a person of sin and turns him to Christ (see John 16:8).

## The only way to live

As comforting as John's words are, they do leave imperfect Christians with feelings of ambivalence. What if there are still unanswered prayers? At least the answers seem to often fall in the "no" or "wait" categories a great deal of the time. What if it is hard to tell just where you should stand on a certain issue to be sure you are "abiding in Christ"?

The "what ifs" whisper to many and roar in the ears of others. The way to block them out is never to confuse abiding in Christ with struggle and effort.

Bruce Larson, who worked for years in New York City as executive director of Faith at Work, would often counsel people who were struggling with tough decisions. When trusting and abiding seemed hard for them to grasp, he would ask them to take a short walk from his office to the RCA building on Fifth

Avenue. There, at the entrance, they would admire the giant statue of Atlas with muscles bulging, straining to hold the world on his powerful shoulders.

"Now, that's one way to live," Larson would say, "trying to carry the world on your shoulders. But now come across the street with me."

On the other side of Fifth Avenue was Saint Patrick's Cathedral, and there behind the high altar Larson would show his companion a small shrine of the boy, Jesus, who was holding the world in one hand with no effort at all.

The point was always made. As Larson writes, "We have a choice. We can carry the world on our shoulders or we can say, 'I give up, Lord, here's my life. I give you my world, the whole world.'"[13]

## *Test Your Faith*

A French proverb tells us, "There is no pillow so soft as a clear conscience."[14] This chapter has dealt with a section of John's letter that puts strong emphasis on doing the loving thing instead of just talking about it. According to John, what we actually do, think and say has a powerful effect on our conscience.

The following questions are designed to help you rate your Christian life-style and motivations on a scale of 1 to 10. On the "1" side of the scale you have the extreme negative; on the "10" side of the scale you have the extreme positive. Where do you fall?

1. My life-style (what I actually do, think and say) reflects:

     1    2    3    4    5    6    7    8    9    10

     Cain and hatred                    Christ and love

2. If others would describe my Christian witness and ministry, they would say I am:

1   2   3   4   5   6   7   8   9   10

A talker                                A doer

3. I share my possessions with others:

1   2   3   4   5   6   7   8   9   10

Seldom                              Constantly

4. I spend my time:

1   2   3   4   5   6   7   8   9   10

Mostly on                          Mostly on
myself                                others

5. I pass the buck:

1   2   3   4   5   6   7   8   9   10

Always                              Never

6. When John writes, "If our hearts condemn us, God is greater than our hearts and He knows everything," I feel:

1   2   3   4   5   6   7   8   9   10

Afraid                              Comforted

7. When I pray, I:

1   2   3   4   5   6   7   8   9   10

Don't seem to                Always get an
get many                        answer
answers

8. My life is best described as:

1   2   3   4   5   6   7   8   9   10

All struggle                    Total trust
and effort                      in Christ

---

## Notes

1. The "Prayer of Saint Francis" has been ascribed to the Catholic saint who lived from 1182-1226. According to Lawrence Cunningham, ed., *Brother Francis: An Anthology of Writings By and About St. Francis of Assisi* (New York: Harper & Row Pubs., Inc., 1972). p. 21, this prayer was actually written by an unknown person who lived during the twentieth century.
2. 1 John 3:18, *The Living Bible.*
3. John Stott, *The Epistles of John* (Grand Rapids: Wm B. Eerdmans Publishing Co., 1960), p. 136, where he quotes David Smith from *The Expositor's Greek Testament Commentary on the Epistles of John.*
4. The Greek word John uses is *esphaxen* which, according to Robert Law, *The Test of Life* (Grand Rapids: Baker Book House, 1968), p. 239, originally meant to "kill by cutting the throat." The idea behind the word, says Law, is one of brutal slaughter. The idea of brutal slaughter is also suggested by Genesis 4:10 when the Lord says, "Your brother's blood cries out to me from the ground."
5. Charles Colson, *Loving God* (Grand Rapids: Zondervan Publishing House, 1983), p. 32.
6. For the full account of this moving story, see Colson, *Loving God,* pp. 27-34.
7. John may also be recalling Jesus' words from the Sermon on the Mount, where He equated angry hatred with murder (see Matt. 5:21,22).
8. Accounts of one twin donating a kidney to the other are not unusual. Exact details on this story are unknown.
9. Colson, *Loving God,* chap. 14, "The Everyday Business of Holiness," especially pp. 131-133.
10. Lee Buck with Dick Schneider, *Tapping Your Secret Source of Power* (Old Tappan, NJ: Fleming H. Revell Co., 1985). pp. 53-57.
11. Stott, *The Epistles of John* p. 148.

12. James Boice, *The Epistles of John* (Grand Rapids: Zondervan Publishing House, 1979), pp. 126, 127, where he quotes C. H. Dodd, *Johannine Epistles,* p. 93.
13. Bruce Larson, *Believe and Belong* (Old Tappan, NJ: Fleming H. Revell Co., 1982), p. 21.
14. Eleanor Doan, *Speaker's Sourcebook* (Grand Rapids: Zondervan Publishing House, 1960), p. 67.

# 10

# How Can You Tell If It's Really "The Spirit"?

*Great is the truth, and in the end it will prevail.*[1]
—*Latin Proverb*

*Dearly beloved friends, don't always believe everything you hear just because someone says it is a message from God: test it first to see if it really is. For there are many false teachers around.*[2]
—*The Apostle John*

According to an ancient manuscript written by John's disciple, Prochorus, the apostle encountered a pagan magician, Kynops, on the island of Patmos. A large crowd was present and Kynops asked a young man in the multitude where his father was. The youth replied that his father's ship had gone down in a storm and he was dead.

Kynops turned to John, "Come, bring up the young man's father from the dead."

John gazed steadily into Kynops's eyes and replied evenly, "I have not come to raise the dead, but to deliver the living from their errors."

The scholars have trouble verifying stories like this, but this one definitely has a ring of truth about it. Battling pagan errors was one of John's chief priorities and a major reason why he wrote his Epistles.[3] When John wrote his first letter, Christianity was being threatened by its pagan neighbors in one of two ways:

> *One.* Other religions and philosophies would like certain elements of the Christian faith and would pick and choose some of these for their own use, while discarding the views they didn't like.
>
> *Two.* In the case of the Gnostics, they didn't pick and choose from Christian beliefs to "spice up" their own religious viewpoint. Rather, they moved in on Christianity and tried to influence it from within with their own pagan ideas.

John has already taken the Gnostics to task once for their denial of the deity of Jesus (see 2:18-27). In that portion of his letter he zeroed in on the Gnostics by calling them junior antichrists, forerunners of the real antichrist who is yet to appear.

John's word of warning to Christians is capped by his words of encouragement about their being anointed with the Holy Spirit who would help them discern between those who deny the Son and those who acknowledge Him (see 2:23).

At the end of chapter 2 of his letter, and on through chapter 3, John moves into his second round of tests of a Christian. In 2:28–3:10 he repeats the moral test that asks, "Do I obey?" and finds the Gnostics wanting once more. In 3:11-24 he repeats the social test, "Do I love?", and the Gnostics flunk again, relegated to keeping company with none other than Cain, history's first murderer (see 3:12-15).

As John closes chapter 3 of his letter, he assures Christians by reminding them of how Christ lives within because of the "Spirit he gave us" (3:24). Now John will repeat his doctrinal test, "Do I believe?", as he warns against false spirits who teach lies about Jesus Christ.

### 1 John 4:1-3

Dear friends, do not believe every spirit, but test the spirits to see whether they are from God, because many false prophets have gone out into the world. This is how you can recognize the Spirit of God: Every Spirit that acknowledges that Jesus Christ has come in the flesh is from God, but every spirit that does not acknowledge Jesus is not from God. This is the spirit of the antichrist, which you have heard is coming and even now is already in the world.

John is taking the trouble to give his readers a second warning about doctrinal dangers for at least two reasons: (1) Nothing is more important than a person's view of Jesus Christ. Get that wrong and everything else is academic; (2) The churches John was writing to had wide-open, free-spirited worship services that were tailor-made for Gnostic infiltration.

There was a "super-charged, spirit-filled atmosphere" in the early churches.[4] Sign gifts such as prophecy and tongues were prevalent, as well as other supernatural phenomena. In addition, the informal nature of a typical worship service made it easy for visitors to get up and say their piece. Naturally, the Gnostic false teachers who were circulating throughout the area took full advantage of this kind of opportunity.

## The supernatural is not always divine

John's warning in verse 1, "Do not believe every spirit," is a strong implication that many members of the early Church were swallowing just about anything that was said in the service as long as it seemed to be inspired. What these undiscerning Christians needed to realize was that there is a big difference between the supernatural and the divine.[5]

Of course, the need to tell true from false spirits was nothing new in the early Church. In 1 Corinthians 12:10, Paul wrote about those who had the gift to "distinguish between spirits." But here in his Epistle, John doesn't seem to be talking about individuals who have a special gift. He refers to a general ability possessed by all Christians. Paul says the same thing in 1 Thessalonians 5:21,22: "Test everything. Hold on to the good. Avoid every kind of evil."

Every Christian is obligated to be discerning in what he listens to and believes in. And every believer has this ability, which is available through the anointing of the Spirit that John talked about back in 1 John 2:20, 27, as well as 3:24.[6] We have the responsibility to be aware that other spirits are active in the world and that eloquence, fervor and even the manipulation of Scripture verses don't necessarily prove that someone is speaking for God.

How are the Christians supposed to tell the real thing from the false? John says, "You can test whether they come from God in this simple way: Every spirit that acknowledges the fact that Jesus Christ actually became man, comes from God, but the spirit which denies this fact does not come from God: The latter comes from the anti-Christ, which you were warned would come and which is already in the world" (1 John 4:2,3, *Phillips*).

When John talks about "testing" he uses the same Greek word *dokimazo* that was employed in ancient times to refer to the testing of metals for genuineness. The idea behind this word is to test something with the expectation of approving it. The same word is used in Luke 14:19 about a man who is going to test or prove some oxen.

All this suggests that Christians shouldn't turn into head-hunters who are trying to find fault in everything that is said in a church service. In keeping with his emphasis to love one another, John suggests that Christians test teachings, testimonies, prophetic utterances, etc., with the hope and desire that they may prove correct.

"Be on the lookout for false prophets," says John, "but don't get paranoid about it."

The best way to escape spiritual paranoia or spiritual naiveté is to personally know the living Word of God and to know the written Word that talks about His deity. One basic test of any spirit is to see if the teaching honors the Son of God. Jesus made it very clear that the Holy Spirit's specific ministry was to testify to and glorify Him (see John 15:26; 16:13-15).

When John refers to the spirits who acknowledge Jesus Christ has come in the flesh (see 1 John 4:2) and spirits that don't (see v. 3), he has to be thinking about his old Gnostic nemesis, Cerinthus, who denied the incarnation with cunning subtlety. Like any counterfeit teacher who tries to make his words sound genuine, Cerinthus didn't come right out and say, "Look, we all know that all matter is evil and that God could never become matter. Therefore, Jesus Christ couldn't possibly be God."

What Cerinthus *did* say was something like this: "The heavenly Christ entered into Jesus at His baptism but He didn't stay permanently. He empowered Jesus to give wonderful teachings but left Him before the crucifixion. Jesus was still a powerful teacher of God's truth which was proved by His resurrection following His death."

Spiritual counterfeits will always grant certain points as long as they can make other vital ones that are more crucial and basic. But what the Gnostics like Cerinthus would never admit is that God actually became a man. As John had said in his Gospel, the *logos*—God Himself—became flesh to dwell among us (see John 1:14).

## Plenty of false spirits are still around

In chapter 7 of this book we took a brief look at the Jehovah's Witnesses, a group that has much in common with the Gnostics. One thing that can be said for the Jehovah's Witnesses is that they are straightforward: They make no bones about denying Christ's deity and the Trinity.

But another organization, which may be growing even faster than the Witnesses, is much harder to pin down. This cult also works its way through neighborhoods just like yours and usually arrives at your front door on 10-speed bikes in the form of two polite young men, neatly attired in white shirt and tie. The Mormons—the Church of Jesus Christ of Latter-day Saints—ask two years of missionary service from their young men, who are carefully schooled in Mormon doctrine, given their elder badge and sent out to "evangelize the Gentiles"—all those who are unaware of the "real truth" discovered by Joseph Smith in the early 1800s.

Mormon missionaries are carefully schooled in the fine art of semantics. Dr. Walter Martin, who has spent much of his life studying and refuting Mormon theology, points out Mormons love to use biblical terminology that makes them look as if they are in absolute agreement with the foundational truths of Christianity. In actuality, when they use terms like *God, Jesus Christ, the Lord, heavenly Father,* etc., they have their own definitions of these terms which are far different from those of the orthodox Christian.[7]

James Bjornstad, the cults specialist quoted at length on the Jehovah's Witnesses in chapter 7, advises that the most important question you can ask any religion to see if it is genuinely Christian is *not,* "Do you believe in Jesus Christ?" The first article of faith for the Mormons states that they believe in "His Son, Jesus Christ." Bjornstad believes a better question is the same one Christ asked the Pharisees in Matthew 22:42: "What do you think about the Christ?"

What Mormons think about Christ is this:

> • Jesus is a created being, the "firstborn spirit child" in a long line of children sexually conceived in

spirit form by a heavenly Father who is the God of the universe. According to the Mormons, all people who have ever lived on earth were born first in a spirit form in heaven.

• In the spirit world Jesus had a brother named Lucifer. The heavenly Father chose Jesus to be Saviour of the world but Lucifer thought he could do it better. There was an argument and Lucifer rebelled, taking one-third of the existing spirits in heaven with him. They became Satan and his demons.

• Jesus was born of Mary but He was not conceived by Joseph nor was He conceived by the Holy Ghost. A heavenly Father, God of flesh and bones, had sexual relations with Mary.

• Mormons believe Jesus was married, perhaps to as many women as Mary, Martha and Mary Magdalene. Jesus had children by all of His wives.

• Jesus became a god through consistent obedience to all of the gospel and the law. He is the model, or standard, of salvation for Mormons. Just as Jesus became a god, all male Mormons can become gods through hard work and obedience to the Law. A female Mormon cannot attain godhood, however; she simply goes along for the ride if her husband becomes a god.

All of the above teachings by the Mormons on the Person of Jesus Christ are carefully documented by Bjornstad in his book, *Counterfeits at Your Door.*[8]

The above are just a few examples of Mormon heresy. As with Jehovah's Witnesses, literature describing the contradictory and counterfeit teachings of the Mormons is available in every form from simple to highly complex. They are touched on in this chapter as one more example of false spirits who do not accept the Son of God Himself. Cults like the Jehovah's Witnesses and Mormons are obvious examples of the false spirits John mentions in 1 John 4:1-3, but there are many other sources and versions of false spirits that aren't as easy to spot.

## Why "fantasy games" aren't harmless

A recent phenomenon, inventors of which claim is perfectly innocent fun in the tradition of C. S. Lewis's *Narnia Tales,* is the Fantasy Role Playing games (F.R.P. games) such as Dungeons and Dragons®, Tunnels and Trolls, and Arduin Grimoire. In their well-researched book *Playing with Fire,* James Bjornstad and John Weldon discuss the obvious dangers in F.R.P. games, which have taken the nation by storm since being introduced on college campuses in 1975.[9]

The millions of fans and supporters of games like Dungeons and Dragons® (D & D) claim they are nothing more than a harmless excursion into the fantasy and imagination, no worse than chess and better than Monopoly. D & D® has been called an educational tool that helps players become more creative and assertive, no more harmful than Tolkien fantasy, but more interesting and captivating. Opponents of F.R.P. games charge that D & D® is a demonic, pagan, witch-loving game of the devil, the most effective, the most magnificently packaged, the most profitably marketed, the most thoroughly researched introduction to the occult in recorded history.[10]

According to Bjornstad and Weldon, the lack of a real moral viewpoint, plus obvious references to and promotions of the occult, make F.R.P. games highly dangerous. In Dungeons and Dragons®, for example, there is a battle between "good" and "evil" but there are no moral absolutes or moral conclusions. There is no attempt to have "good" triumph over "evil" in the end. While you are playing the game, "good" is actually no better than "evil". While engaging in his game playing, the fantasy role player lives in an "amoral universe" where the end justifies the means.

Can Christians play Dungeons and Dragons® without harm? Depending on the role they choose, players may have to engage in prostitution, theft, mutilation of enemies, rape, human sacrifice, necromancy (communicating with the dead), astral projection (soul travel), and the summoning of demons and devils. If they progress to playing advanced Dungeons and Dragons®, serving one of the "gods" is a basic part of the game.[11]

While F.R.P. games have no direct connection to the

Gnostics, there are obvious overtones. The Gnostics believed in "other gods" that included an alternate creator of the earth called a "demi-urge," who was a remote emanation from the true God.[12] Their view of Jesus as a phantom who left no footprints or as a human being who received mysterious heavenly powers for a short time, would fit in nicely with fantasy role-playing concepts.

John confronted the fantasy-laden ideas of the Gnostics head-on. He underscored again and again that Jesus was not simply a man who had an experience that gave Him temporary super powers which were taken away later. When Jesus was born a tiny babe in Bethlehem He was every bit the "God-Man" that He was at age 33. John Stott puts it well: "The fundamental Christian doctrine which can never be compromised is the eternal divine-human Person of Jesus Christ, the Son of God."[13]

Here in chapter 4, John is saying the same thing he said in chapter 2, but in a little different way. In 2:22-25 John taught that those who deny the Son are also denying the Father. In 4:1-3 John teaches that those who deny the Son are without the Holy Spirit as well. To sum up, false teachers, like the Gnostics, *have no part of the Triune God whatsoever.*

How can believers cope with a pagan system that denies and undercuts the deity of Christ at every turn? John goes on to explain why the victory is already won:

### 1 John 4:4-6

You, dear children, are from God and have overcome them, because the one who is in you is greater than the one who is in the world. They are from the world and therefore speak from the viewpoint of the world, and the world listens to them. We are from God, and whoever knows God listens to us; but whoever is not from God does not listen to us. This is how we recognize the Spirit of truth and the spirit of falsehood.

As he gives warnings and occasional admonishments, John never fails to include encouragement and assurance. Christians who keep the deity of Christ—incarnation of God—central in their doctrinal beliefs have nothing to fear from heretics. The false teacher of heresy is representative of the powers of evil, and Christ has already dealt those powers a deathblow at the Cross. In verse 4, John reminds believers that the One who is in them (the Holy Spirit) is far greater than the "one who is in the world" (Satan).

As he did in chapter 2, John practically identifies the world (the pagan system of unbelief and rebellion against God) with the false teachers of heresy. For all practical purposes they are one and the same. As J. B. Phillips puts it: "The agents of the anti-Christ are children of the world, they speak the world's language and the world pays attention to what they say" (v. 5).

When studying verse 6, it helps to sort out whom John is referring to with his pronouns. When he says, "We are from God," he means apostles like himself or other teachers of God's truth. When he says, "Whoever knows God," he means God's people—those who recognize God's Word and accept it. John is making an obvious but powerful point: You can always recognize God's Word because people listen to it; and you can always recognize God's people because they listen to His word.[14]

It's important to note that John is doing much more here than belaboring the obvious. He is describing how the Holy Spirit works in Christ's Body—the community of believers. He is underscoring the strength of Christian fellowship. Christians are not to operate as individuals who think they don't need anybody else. The best place to "test the spirits" is in the company of other Christians, where they can encourage and love one another.

John started his letter by saying he wanted to proclaim what he had seen, heard and touched in order that all his readers might have fellowship with him (see 1:3,4). The power of fellowship—Christians standing shoulder to shoulder, arm and arm, and hand in hand *with one another*—has never been completely tapped by the Church from John's day until the present.

### The invaluable resources of the "one anothers"

Scripture is full of instructions on what Christians should (or should not) do to and for one another. In *Reciprocal Living,* author Sue Harville discusses 25 "one another" statements which she calls "reciprocal commands for Christians." When anything is "reciprocal" it suggests two-way action between parties. Harville divides the 25 one-another statements into four groups:

1. How to get along with one another.
2. What not to do to each other.
3. How to build each other up.
4. How to serve one another.[15]

All of the reciprocal commands are worth careful study. But the ones dealing with building the Body (mutual edification) are particularly useful in our look at 1 John 4:1-6, which emphasizes telling true spirits from false and overcoming the world. Webster defines *edify* as "to build, establish, improve or enlighten." A secondary definition is: "to instruct and improve the mind of, particularly morally or spiritually."

In the New Testament, the Greek word for edify is *oikodomeo,* which literally has to do with building a house. It is used throughout the New Testament in a metaphorical sense to mean the promoting of spiritual growth in the development of character of believers by teaching or by example.[16]

When describing how Christians can edify one another, the New Testament speaks of the following:

- Building up one another (see Rom 14:19; 1 Thess. 5:11)
- Teaching one another (see Col. 3:16)
- Exhorting (encouraging) one another (see 1 Thess. 5:11; Heb. 3:13)
- Admonishing (counseling) one another (see Rom. 15:14; Col. 3:16)
- Speaking to one another in psalms, hymns and spiritual songs (see Eph. 5:19; Col. 3:16).

All of the above ideas overlap and blend with one another to

some extent. If you wanted to find one verse that would sum up
the concept of mutual edification, you could do no better than
Colossians 3:16:

> Let the word of Christ dwell in you richly as you
> teach and admonish one another with all wisdom,
> and as you sing psalms, hymns and spiritual  songs
> with gratitude in your hearts to God.

What better way than this to discern true spirits from false
and to overcome the world? But if these qualities are missing
from a Christian fellowship, it can lead to a *"koinonia* crisis"—
and susceptibility to counterfeits, heretics and false spirits that
crowd in from every side.

In six brief verses—1 John 4:1-6—the apostle completes his
second complete round of tests that ask the Christian three
basic questions:

- Do you obey?
- Do you love?
- Do you believe?

In 1 John 4:7–5:3 he will cover these three questions again,
but in a different way. He will focus on love more intensely than
ever as his letter rises to new heights. Only in 1 John 4 do we
find the profound statement, "God is love" and its encouragement for imperfect Christians who seek to be complete
Christ.

## Test Your Faith

Testing the spirits to see whether they were true or false
was a major concern in John's day. Is it still a concern in the
twentieth century? Answer the following questions to test your
own awareness.

1. When someone at church comes up with a different opinion on a theological issue, I:

    __a.  Immediately question his salvation

    __b.  Become a bit fearful or suspicious

    __c.  Am open to new ideas.

2. For me, having correct doctrine is:

    __a.  Not too important. "No creed but Christ" is a good motto.

    __b.  Important, but it's how you live that really counts.

    __c.  The foundation on which I build my Christian faith and life.

3. When John writes about the Christian's responsibility to "test the spirits," I:

    __a.  Am not too sure I know what he's talking about

    __b.  Am not too sure I know enough about the Bible

    __c.  Feel confident I can recognize false doctrine when I hear it.

4. If Mormon missionaries came to my door, I would:

    __a.  Ask them why women can't attain godhood

    __b.  Ask them who Jesus' Father was

    __c.  Ask them to explain how they know they are going to heaven, then give my own testimony.

5. The suggestion that fantasy role-playing games like Dungeons and Dragons® can be an example of false spirits sounds to me like:

    __a.  Stretching things a bit

    __b.  Something to be concerned about

    __c.  Something to fear and avoid.

6. This chapter claims that the best place to "test the spirits" is in the company of other Christians where you can encourage and love one another. Do you:

    __a.  Wish it were so in your case

___b.   Agree in principle

___c.   Know from experience this is true?

7. The most important way Christians can edify (build up) one another is:

___a.   Teach one another

___b.   Encourage one another

___c.   Admonish one another.

Write a brief paragraph explaining your choice.

## Notes

1. Quoted by William Barclay, *The Letters of John and Jude* Daily Study Bible (Edinburgh: The St. Andrew Press, 1958), p. 112.

2. 1 John 4:1, *The Living Bible.*

3. Alfred Plummer, *The Epistles of St. John* (Cambridge: The University Press, 1911), p. 7.

4. Herschel H. Hobbs, *The Epistles of John* (Nashville: Thomas Nelson, Inc., 1983), p. 97.

5. George C. Findlay, *Fellowship in the Life Eternal* (an exposition of *The Epistles of St. John*) (Hodder & Stoughton, 1909), quoted by John Stott, *The Epistles of John* (Grand Rapids: Wm. B. Eerdmans Publishing Co., 1960), p. 152.

6. Curtis Vaughn, *1, 2, 3 John* (Grand Rapids: Zondervan Publishing House, 1970), p. 91.

7. Walter Martin, *The Maze of Mormonism* (Ventura, CA: Vision House, 1962), pp. 269-272.

8. James Bjornstad *Counterfeits at Your Door* (Ventura, CA: Regal Books, 1979), pp. 110-112; also his documentation on p. 116.

9. James Bjornstad and John Weldon, *Playing with Fire* (Chicago: Moody Press, 1984), p. 17. Sales of F.R.P. games rose from $150,000 in 1975 to an estimated $150 million in 1982.

10. Ibid., p. 22.

11. Ibid., especially chapts. 4, "Black, White, or a Mixture of Greys?" and 5, "The Occult Connection," pp. 45-77.

12. Kenneth Scott Latourette, *The History of the Expansion of Christianity, The First Five Centuries* (Grand Rapids: Zondervan Publishing House, 1970), pp. 338, 339. Originally published by Harper & Row Pubs., Inc. (New York: 1937).

13. Stott, *The Epistles of John* p. 154.

14. Ibid., p. 158.

15. Sue Harville, *Reciprocal Living* (Coral Gables, FL: Learning Resource Center, World Team, 1976), p. 24.

16. W. E. Vine, *Vine's Expository Dictionary of New Testament Words* (Old Tappan, NJ: Fleming H. Revell Co., 1981), p. 18.

# 11

# Has Anyone Seen God Lately?

*If a thing is worth doing, it is worth doing poorly.*[1]
—G. K. Chesterton

*No one has ever seen God; but if we love
each other, God lives in us and his love is
made complete in us.*[2]
—The Apostle John

Another tale of tradition tells us that in John's final days he grew so weak he had to be carried into the church. The faithful gathered around to hear a word from their beloved leader, and that word, was always the same, "Little children, love one another."

While everyone in the church held the aged apostle in the highest esteem and respect, some people got a bit tired of always hearing John say those same words. Finally, someone asked, "Master, why do you always speak thus?"

John replied, "Because it is the Lord's command, and if only this be done, it is enough."[3]

That certainly does sound like John. It especially sounds like the next passage of his letter, which scholars have called one of the mountain peaks of the New Testament.

As we have seen, John's writing is not carefully structured, but his Epistle does have a plan. He has already presented two cycles of "tests of the true Christian." Each time he has touched three main nerves to expose the heresies of the Gnostics who: (1) did not obey (the moral test); (2) did not love (the social test); (3) did not believe in the Son (the doctrinal test). John finished his second cycle of tests in 4:1-6 with a withering attack on false spirits—the Gnostic prophets who denied the incarnation.

As John begins his third cycle of tests he injects a new tone and a new emphasis that will be a unique combination of doctrine and practical Christian living (believing and loving). John has already written two great truths about the nature of God. In his Gospel he taught, "God is spirit" (John 4:24). Earlier in this Epistle he taught, "God is light" (1 John 1:5). Now he is ready to share the most sublime thought of all, "God is love."

**1 John 4:7-12**

Dear friends, let us love one another, for love comes from God. Everyone who loves has been born of God and knows God. Whoever does not love does not know God, because God is love. This is how God showed his love among us: He sent his one and only Son into the world that we might live through him. This is love: not that we loved God, but that he loved us and sent his Son as an atoning sacrifice for our sins. Dear friends, since God so loved us, we also ought to love one another. No one has ever seen God; but if we loved each other, God lives in us and his love is made complete in us.

John seems to be at his black-and-white best in verses 7 and 8. At first glance his words appear to say: "A real Christian never fails to show love." John's logic is progressively simple: (1) Love comes from God; (2) If you love, you know God; (3) If you don't love, you don't know God, because God *is* love.

But does God demand that a Christian never fail? We have already studied several verses that teach the contrary (see 1 John 1:8-10, 2:1,2). God prefers that we live sinless lives, but He provides the means of cleansing for times when we don't.

## We are a part of the One who is perfect

Verses 7 and 8 aren't saying a real Christian never fails to show love. John is well aware that no Christian is perfect, but he is trying to tell his readers that every Christian is part and parcel with the One who is perfect in every respect. The real Christian may fail on occasion to show love, but the real Christian is always being primed, urged and empowered by the Holy Spirit to demonstrate God's nature, which is love.

*The Amplified Bible* puts verse 7 even more strongly: "He who loves [his fellowmen] is begotten (born) of God and is coming (progressively) to know *and* understand God—to perceive and recognize and get a better and clearer knowledge of Him."

To put it in a simple analogy: I may love to play the game of golf or tennis, but as I participate I often make errors and fail to shoot par or get in my second serve. Nonetheless, I always come back again because I love the game and I want to learn how to play it better and better. However, if I participate in golf and tennis with no regard for the rules nor have an interest in really playing the game as it is designed to be played, I am a phony. In the same way, if I consistently act in a loveless way, with no desire or outward sign of wanting to demonstrate the nature of the One I claim to call Father, I am not a Christian at all.

The above insights are helpful, but if we are honest, "God is love" is still a rather abstract phrase that paints no specific picture in our minds. Perhaps John senses this, for in his next breath he gives a concrete image that immediately comes into focus. God showed His love by sending His Son to be the atoning sacrifice (propitiation) for our sins. Note, God didn't send His Son because of all the love the human race was showing for Him. He sent His one and only Son strictly out of sacrificial love. He sought our good at His own ultimate expense, with no demands that we love Him in return. If we want to return God's love, it is by our choice—not His demand.

## What kind of "love" is John talking about?

Before we go on with John's thoughts about God and love, it might be helpful to understand the kind of love the apostle has in mind. The Greek language, in which John wrote his letter, has three major words for love, all with different meanings: *eros, phileo and agape.*[4]

*Eros* was the word for love that pagan Greeks of John's day would understand the best. To us, *eros* suggests sex or romance and we immediately think of our own word *erotic.* At its base, however, *eros* refers to human self-centeredness. *Eros* means to grasp, reach out and achieve your own satisfaction by acquiring the object (or person) you desire.[5]

It is not too hard to see how sex would fit in with this description. As we saw in chapter 1 of this book, sex was often part of pagan Greek religions. The word the Greeks used for love was almost always *eros.*

*Phileo* is another Greek word for love, but here the emphasis in on "brotherly love." Phileo love is friendship love which is founded on mutual liking. Friendship love automatically suggests a certain amount of selectivity on both sides. When Matthew recorded Jesus' instructions to "love your enemies" (Matt. 5:44), he did not use the word, *phileo*. He used another word—the same one John used throughout his entire Epistle of 1 John—*agape*.

The pagan Greeks had the word *agape* in their vocabulary, but seldom used it. They much preferred *eros*, because it fit in with their religious philosophies much better.

Writers of New Testament books certainly didn't want to identify God's love with the self-centered concepts of *eros*, so it's no surprise that we don't find *eros* appearing even once in the New Testament. What New Testament writers needed was a "word to describe the indescribable."[6] They adapted *agape*, "the most colorless word for 'love' in the Greek vocabulary, in order to express the new moral demands of the Christian faith."[7] In the New Testament the word *agape* reaches far beyond *eros* or *phileo* to describe love that is totally unselfish, totally unconditional and totally sacrificial.

Naturally, the use of *agape* in New Testament writings did not impress the pagan Greeks. They much preferred *eros* to describe religious longings for salvation. But the absolutely critical difference was this: For the Greeks, God didn't provide salvation, they provided salvation for themselves. God didn't have to come down to them; they could rise up to God. They believed their problem wasn't sin; it was simply their humanity—being trapped in a human body. Release man's spirit from his body, said the Greeks, and he will rise to heaven under his own power to be accepted by God as the divine being he really is.

John and other writers of the New Testament taught the precise opposite. In *agape* love they showed God coming down to rescue sinful man, who had no hope within himself. According to the New Testament, man's problem isn't his body, it is his sinful nature. The New Testament teaches that the body is good, deserving and destined for resurrection. The cross of Christ is man's only chance to save his spirit and his body (see 1 Cor. 15:12-58).

The *agape* of the New Testament and the *eros* of pagan Greek religions stood as far apart as the east from the west—possibly farther. Author Michael Harper writes:

> Agape brooks no rivals. It coexists with no one. In the Old Testament the greatest sin that God's people committed was syncretism. The Bible word for it is idolatry. It is the desire to have the best of both worlds, to worship and serve God and other gods. To have *agape* and *eros* is impossible. They don't mix. They start from opposite positions and have totally different objectives.[8]

It is no wonder that the Greeks called the cross of Christ foolishness (1 Cor. 1:18). And as for the resurrection of the body, who needed *that*? For the Greeks the body was evil, something that was part of the material world from which they longed to escape.

John's answer is simple and direct. Everyone needs the Cross and the hope of resurrection (see 1 John 2:2). As John thought about the Gnostic heresy that was infiltrating the Christian Church, he had the battle between *eros* (man's love for himself) and *agape* (God's love for man) clearly in mind. It is no wonder that he emphasized, "This is love: not that we loved God, but that he loved us and sent his Son as an atoning sacrifice for our sins" (4:10). John realized that the difference between *eros* and *agape* wasn't one of degree. It was one of kind. *Agape* and *eros* simply could not coexist. *Eros* was anathema to *agape* and vice versa. *Eros* and *agape* are locked in mortal combat.

One of John's major goals, if not *the* major goal of his letter, is to convince his Christian readers that once your doctrine goes down the wrong road, everything else goes along with it. If you start concentrating on yourself and what you can do for yourself (*eros*), you can have no real love for others. You might make a pretense, but your basic motive betrays you. Self-love is always just that, no matter how much it is dressed up to look like something else.

## When the "oughts" and "shoulds" make sense

While God doesn't demand that we love Him back, He does present us with the opportunity—and the obligation. In verse 11, John makes it clear that "since God loved us, we also ought to love one another." Is John fair in saying we *ought* to do this? "Ought" is first cousin to "should" and psychologists, including many Christian counselors, caution their clients to stop "shoulding" themselves so much.[9] One of the chief sources of neurotic or false guilt is the line that plays the same message over and over in the mind: "I *should* have done that. I *ought* to do this!"

A cartoon character that most people can identify with is Ziggy, the lovable little fellow who deals with life as "it really is." In one Ziggy episode, he spots water dripping from the ceiling and says, "I should fix the roof." Then he spots the dirty floor and comments, "I should give the floor a good scrub." He goes through the house, noting that he *should* fix the cracked plaster, *should* clean out the closet and that he *should* use his time better. In the final frame he reclines in an easy chair saying, "I should stop 'shoulding' myself."[10]

We understand Ziggy's feelings precisely. It is easy to become paralyzed by false guilt, get discouraged and finally depressed because we have so many shoulds and oughts hounding us from every side:

- "I should have said something for the Lord."
- "I ought to go to the meeting, headache or not."
- "I ought to love Mrs. Smith, but she is so impossible!"

Without question, a lot of the shoulds and oughts we dump on ourselves are unnecessary and unhealthy. When we bring God into it, the guilt can mount in a hurry. Paul the apostle knew the feeling and described it in graphic terms in Romans chapter 7: "I do not understand what I do. For what I want to do I do not do, but what I hate I do" (v. 15). Paul found a law or principle at work that never failed to foul him up everytime he wanted to do good (see Rom. 7:21). He was a "prisoner of the law of sin at work within" (v. 23). Paul ends chapter 7 on the brink of despair: "What a wretched man I am! Who will rescue me from this body of death?" (v. 24).

Could part of Paul's problem have been instances of failure to love certain Christian brethren as God had loved him? He doesn't list specifics in Romans 7, but even a casual reading of his letters shows he didn't get along perfectly with everyone.[11] The shoulds and the oughts closed in on Paul just as they do on us.

What is the answer for Paul—and for us? "Thanks be to God—through Jesus Christ our Lord! . . . there is now no condemnation for those who are in Christ Jesus" (Rom. 7:25; 8:1). Paul realizes that false guilt has no power over him. He has obligations to God, true, but he need not wallow in false guilt because he cannot meet them perfectly.

Paul has discovered the great paradox of Christian living: Salvation is a free gift from God, but God still has His list of oughts and shoulds. We can't earn our way to heaven, but there are commands God wants us to obey. John has been pounding home two of those commands throughout his letter: Believe in the Son, and love one another (see 1 John 3:23; 2:3-11). When John says we "ought to love one another" in verse 11, he is using the same Greek word (*opheilomen*) that he uses in 1 John 3:16, 4:11 and 3 John 8. In each case the idea of "owing a debt" is present.

And so we see the paradox in God's *agape* love for us. He loves us unconditionally. He demands no love in return. Yet, every Christian owes Him a debt. Every Christian is obligated to God. But we are not to pay our debt to God out of guilt or fear. We are to pay out of gratitude and love, because He first loved us.

From his conclusion in verse 11 that we ought to love each other, John moves to a mind-boggling thought in verse 12: As we love each other, God's love is made perfect in us!

Note John's first words in verse 12: "No one has ever seen God." The Lord told Moses that "no one may see me and live" (Exod. 33:20). John wrote in his Gospel that no one had ever seen God but that the Son had made Him known (see John 1:18). And again, in John 5:37, Jesus said that the Father had sent Him because "you have never heard his voice nor seen his form."

No wonder John says we ought to love one another. We cannot see God but *God is seen in us* as we love one another. Imperfect as we are, God is working in us "to will and to act according to his good purpose" (Phil. 2:13).

All this sounds like lovely theory, but how does it work? How do we pull it off as we live our human, imperfect lives?

First, we must remember that the Greek word for perfect (*teleios*) means "finished, complete or mature" and not a matter of never making an error. The idea behind *teleios* is growing and becoming, not living flawlessly.

We see God's love being perfected when a young, unmarried Christian gets pregnant but refuses to have an abortion.

We see God's love being perfected when a Christian wife obeys her unsaved husband's unreasonable demands in order to win him to Christ.

We see God's love being perfected when parents of a rebellious teenager never quit loving him or praying for him. We see God's love being perfected every time Christians take risks, every time they sacrifice time, money or ego in the name of Christ. We see God's love being perfected every time Christians act on what they know is right instead of waiting until conditions are more favorable, or they are fully qualified or experienced to do the job.

## Many things are worth doing poorly

There is a well-meaning cult of perfectionism that has sprung up across the land. The relentless search for excellence goes on a pace, fired by the familiar motto: "If a thing is worth doing, it is worth doing *well!*" This motto is engrained in most of us from childhood by parents, teachers and coaches. Most of us seek to do our jobs well and expect others to do the same. It is a virtual cornerstone of our entire society.

To be sure, doing a thing well or right is a worthy goal, especially if you are a surgeon, airline pilot or sharpshooter on a police SWAT team. But as with many truisms, there is an inherent problem in the idea of always "doing it well." The problem is this: If we don't think we can do something well, we probably won't even try. Immobilized by fear of embarrassment, we settle for doing nothing. Chesterton was right. There are many things that are worth doing, even if we have to do them poorly (i.e., less than perfectly).

Opportunities to do worthwhile things poorly are everywhere. We can all make our own lists, such as:

- Comforting the mother who just lost her baby, even if "we never seem to know what to say"
- Saying a word for Christ to those sophisticated neighbors
- Teaching a Sunday School class, even if we don't "feel qualified"
- Leading in prayer (or just taking part in conversational prayer), despite our uncertainty about what "sounds good"
- Being firm but loving with an impossible teenager who is too big to spank, ground or control in any way
- Being firm but loving with an impossible anybody
- Just saying "I love you" to a spouse, a son, a daughter, a brother or sister in Christ.

Throughout John's letter, and in all the Scriptures, there is an encouraging note: God doesn't demand that we love with great skill and impeccable wisdom. We may not love perfectly or completely. We may not feel very loving as we "go through the required motions." But that doesn't matter. We are simply told to love—as best we can, as much as we can, according to where we are on that scale God calls, "I'm not finished with you yet."

In just a few verses of chapter 4 John has taken us into deep water indeed. And it's going to get deeper! As Nicodemus said to Jesus one night, "How can these things be?" We'll take a special look at this in the next chapter.

## *Test Your Faith*

In this chapter, John stresses that as Christians we are part of the One who is perfect, the One who gave the commandment to love. And if we love, then others will see God in us. Not only are we to love one another, but we are to love God, not because we have to, but because we want to. Answer the following questions to determine your understanding of God's commandment to love and whether or not others see God in you:

1. What is your opinion of the story that opens this chapter? Is "loving one another" all that Christians need to do? What did John mean?

2. How specifically is God seen in me? (See 1 John 4:12.)

3. Do you agree or disagree: "Salvation is a free gift from God, but God still has His list of oughts and shoulds." What Scripture can you cite to back up your answer?

4. Which motto do you like better, and why?

- If a thing is worth doing, it is worth doing well.
- If a thing is worth doing, it is worth doing poorly.

5. What are you leaving undone because you fear you may do it poorly?

## Notes

1. Quoted by Bruce Larson, *Wind and Fire*, (Waco, TX: Word, Inc., 1984), p. 33.
2. 1 John 4:12.
3. Alfred Plummer, *The Epistles of St. John* (Grand Rapids: Baker Book House, 1980, first published 1886), p. xxxv.
4. A fourth Greek term for love is *storge*, which is used to refer to the love or affection existing in family life, particularly between parent and child. There is no specific word in the Old or New Testament for this kind of love. *Storge* is a term

used only in the compound, and then rarely.

5. Curtis Vaughan, *1,2,3 John* (Grand Rapids: Wm. B. Eerdmans Publishing Co., 1970), p. 102.

6. Michael Harper, *The Love Affair* (Grand Rapids: Wm. B. Eerdmans Publishing Co., 1982), p. 63.

7. Ibid., p. 63.

8. Ibid., p. 133.

9. See, for example, an excellent discussion of how "shoulding yourself" produces false guilt and depression in Dave Stoop's *Self Talk: Key to Personal Growth* (Old Tappan, NJ: Fleming H. Revell Co., 1982), pp. 80-84.

10. Ibid., p. 83.

11. See, for example, 1 and 2 Corinthians and 2 Timothy 4.

# 12
# What Is This Thing Called *Agape*?

*How many Christians really believe that it is easier to love men then God? Possibly it is a very small number, for our natural inclination is to think it is easier to love God simply because He is worthy of our love and that it is difficult to love men because they are not lovable or lovely.*[1]
—*James Montgomery Boice*

*We love because he first loved us.*[2]
—*The Apostle John*

As Nicodemus slips through the darkened streets, he wonders: *Are you sure you should be doing this? What if other members of the Sanhedrin find out? Is it worth the risk? But—there is something about this fellow, Jesus—something you have to know!*

In a few moments Nicodemus is with this strange and provocative Rabbi called Jesus and Nicodemus learns far more than he bargained for. His polite and complimentary greeting is answered by a flat declaration: "Nicodemus, you must be born again!"

Nicodemus draws a sharp breath. He knows what Jesus means but he is afraid to admit it. And so he plays for time and replies: "How can a man be born when he is old? Surely he cannot enter a second time into his mother's womb . . . "

Nicodemus hopes this will hold Jesus off. He knows Jesus really isn't talking about physical birth. The Jews—especially the Pharisees—were very familiar with the concept of rebirth. Proselytes who were accepted into Judaism through prayer, sacrifice and baptism were referred to as "reborn." They were called "newborn children." Nicodemus knows what Jesus means by "being born again." In his heart is a great longing—an emptiness. How can he, a supposedly mature Pharisee and a member of the Sanhedrin to boot, make such a drastic change of heart? Nicodemus thinks to himself: "I'd like to change. That's really why I'm here talking to this strange Rabbi. Being born again is necessary, all right, but is it really possible? It seems just about as feasible as reentering my mother's womb and being brought into the world like a tiny babe."

Jesus senses Nicodemus's dilemma. Instead of backing him into a corner, He gives him principles for spiritual life and change that have never been surpassed: "Unless a man is born of . . .

the Spirit, he cannot enter the kingdom of God. Flesh gives birth to flesh, but the Spirit gives birth to spirit."

There is a bit more to the conversation. You can read it all in John 3:1-15. We are never sure Nicodemus understands or wants to accept what Jesus is saying. But some kind of seed was planted that night. We don't hear from Nicodemus again until the final chapters of John's Gospel when he appears with Joseph of Arimathaea to take down the broken and bloody body of Christ from the cross. To identify himself with Jesus' followers undoubtedly cost Nicodemus many friends among the Pharisees. He must have been aware it could have even cost him his life. Yet there he was—in broad, late afternoon daylight—ministering to this one they had crucified.[3]

Was Jesus Nicodemus's lord? Had Nicodemus been born again? Had he gone through the radical change that only the Holy Spirit can achieve within a person's heart and soul? We can only speculate. After helping Joseph of Arimathaea with the burial, Nicodemus slips from the pages of Scripture and his fate is unknown. We wonder. Did John ever think about Nicodemus as he battled the heretics in his later years? It's quite possible, especially as he pens the next paragraph of his letter.

### 1 John 4:13-16

We know that we live in him and he is us, because he has given us of his Spirit. And we have seen and testify that the Father has sent his Son to be the Savior of the world. If anyone acknowledges that Jesus is the Son of God, God lives in him and he in God. And so we know and rely on the love God has for us.

God is love. Whoever lives in love lives in God, and God in him.

## Nothing happens without the Holy Spirit

In 4:7-12, John zeroed in on one more cycle of his social test for every Christian, which asked: "Do you love?" Now, beginning with verse 13 and continuing to the end of chapter 4, he will combine the social test with the doctrinal test. The only way we can love as we ought to love and allow God to perfect His love in us (4:11,12) is through the Holy Spirit within. Every Christian is born again through the Holy Spirit. This is how the Christian knows he lives in God and God lives in him (see v. 13).

What is the proof that the Spirit is within? You confess that the Father sent the Son to be the Saviour of the world (see v. 14). To confess Jesus as the Son of God is to have God live in you and to know that you live in God (see v. 15).

John caps his argument in verse 16 by saying that Christians know and rely on God's love. They know that God is love, and as they live in love they have the evidence they are living in God and that God lives in them.

All of this has a lovely devotional sound, but to understand how it can possibly work you cannot put too much emphasis on verse 13, "We know that we live in him and he in us, because he has given us of his Spirit." Without these words, the magnificence of John's entire "God is love" passage falls apart.[4]

For the Christian, nothing happens without the Holy Spirit. Before salvation, we are blinded by the devil (see 2 Cor. 4:4), and we are in the dark (see Eph. 4:18). But as God draws us to Himself (see John 6:44) and His light shines in our hearts (see 2 Cor. 4:6) we come to call Jesus Lord through the Holy Spirit (see 1 Cor. 12:3).

Once we confess Jesus as Lord and believe in our hearts that God raised Him from the dead (see Rom. 10:9,10), the Holy Spirit enables us to understand God's truth (see 1 Cor. 2:9-16). As we go on toward maturity in Christ (the process of sanctification), it is through the Holy Spirit we are guaranteed or assured that we live in God and He lives in us (see especially *Phillips* translation of 1 John 4:13).

Always, the emphasis is on God's work in our lives through the Holy Spirit. When we acknowledge Jesus as the Son of God, it shows that the Holy Spirit has been at work in us. God lives in us and we live in God. When we live in love, it shows that the Holy Spirit is at work, that we live in God and that God lives in us. The point is this: we believe and love only because God drew us to Himself in the first place when the Holy Spirit invaded our lives with His love and grace. In his matchless narrative, *The*

*Song,* Calvin Miller puts it this way:

> The Great Invader breathes upon you as a man
> Of Holy Fire, from the far land where all
> Horizons meet . . . And penetrates the wall
> Of your resistance . . . [5]

Our resistance is always the problem. God the Great Invader comes in to dwell, but we do not give Him full reign. The flesh battles the spirit in continual warfare (see Gal. 5:17). When the flesh has the upper hand, we know fear and defeat. But when the Spirit fills our lives with love, we realize two precious blessings. John explains those blessings next:

### 1 John 4:17-21

> Love is made complete among us so that we will have confidence on the day of judgment, because in this world we are like him. There is no fear in love. But perfect love drives out fear, because fear has to do with punishment. The man who fears is not made perfect in love.
>
> We love because he first loved us. If anyone says, "I love God," yet hates his brother, he is a liar. For anyone who does not love his brother, whom he has seen, cannot love God, whom he has not seen. And he has given us this command: Whoever loves God must also love his brother.

Fear is a universal experience. At some time, all of us know fear of someone or something.

But where does fear actually come from? Emerson said fear always springs from ignorance. Aristotle observed that fear is pain arising from the anticipation of evil. Franklin Roosevelt calmed Americans during the crises of the '30s and '40s with, "We have nothing to fear but fear itself."

John might have put it this way: "We Christians have nothing to fear but forgetting that God really does love us."

John knew that the best defense of the faith is a good

offense. The best way to conquer fear is with confidence (the Greek actually means "bold assurance"). He has already mentioned the Christian's confidence in two other places in his letter. In 2:28, he urges his readers to continue in Christ in order to be confident when He comes again (or, if death comes first, when they meet Him face to face). In 3:21-24, he speaks of our confidence before God because our hearts (consciences) do not condemn us. In both passages confidence is based on continuing (abiding or living) in God and obeying His command to love.

In 4:17, John mentions for a third time this confidence that comes through abiding in God and His love. *Phillips* translation says it beautifully: "So our love for him grows more and more, filling us with complete confidence for the day when he shall judge all men—for we realize that our life in this world is actually his life lived in us."

Note especially the phrase "grows more and more." Other versions say our love is "made complete" *(NIV)* or "perfected" *(NASB)*.

The idea of continued growth gives the better meaning. John is not saying our love has to be flawless and without error. He is saying our love for God—and one another—will develop and mature as we fix our eyes on Christ.[6]

### Nothing to fear but a lack of faith

There is an inscription over the door of a hotel in England that reads:

> Fear knocked at the door.
> Faith answered.
> No one was there.[7]

John would have liked that sign. Without faith in what God can do, we will not grow into the "perfect" (fully developed and mature) love that drives out fear. *Phillips* translation of verse 18 is useful here also where he says, "Fully-developed love expels every particle of fear, for fear always contains some of the torture of feeling guilty." The Greek word used for "fear" in verse 18 is *phobos,* which means "terror that causes flight."

We have all experienced those times when we think we must flee God because we fear we have not pleased Him. John is saying, however, that as our love for God grows more and more complete, we experience less and less of this terror-stricken fear and more and more of the reverence that builds our trust in Him.

In one sense we should always "fear God" but it should be a wholesome fear. When Paul writes about the work of the Holy Spirit in the life of the Christian, he says, "For you did not receive a spirit that makes you a slave again to fear, but you received the Spirit of sonship. And by him we cry, '*Abba*, Father'" (Rom. 8:15). The idea behind "Abba" is that we can actually call God "Papa" as would a small child who comes in trust to its earthly father.

When God's children are able to say "Abba, Father," love has driven out fear. But when they cannot come to Him with such open trust, their love for God needs more completing and maturing. As John puts it, "The man who fears is not made perfect in love" (1 John 4:18).

## Perfect love casts out hate

As our love for God grows and matures, we not only have confidence before Him; we are able to love our brothers. Verse 19 contains only seven words, but they speak volumes: "We love because he first loved us."

Before trusting Christ we are full of guilt and fear, which must be cast out (see v. 18). When God comes to live within, He brings *agape* love, something totally foreign to us before our birth into God's family. God didn't save us because we were worthy. He saved us because He is *agape*—sacrificial, unconditional love. Now that God dwells within us in the presence of the Holy Spirit, we have the capacity to show *agape* love to others. *Agape* does not depend on warm, erotic feelings we generate within ourselves (*eros*). *Agape* is an act of the will, not of hormones or emotions. Michael Harper writes:

> *Eros* is love for the beautiful. *Agape* is love for the ugly as well as the beautiful. *Eros* is love for the

good. *Agape* loves the bad and evil also. *Eros* is love
for the friendly. *Agape* is love also for one's enemies.
*Eros* arises within man himself, distorted by original
sin, and so can be self-deceiving. *Agape* arises within
the heart of God and has its only source in Him, and
so is pure and uncontaminated by the pride of man.[8]

In verse 20, John implies that if perfect love casts out fear,
perfect love casts out hatred also. As we have seen in many
places in John's letter (particularly 2:7-11), one of the old apostle's major concerns was the hatred and discord being sown by
the elitist Gnostic idea that some men had more spiritual knowledge (and therefore greater value) than others. It's only logical
then that John would conclude his "God is love" discourse by
pointing out the utter hypocrisy in anyone saying he loves God
while hating his brother (see 4:20).

What John says next gives food for a great deal of thought: If
I cannot love my brother whom I can see, how can I claim I love
God whom I have never seen? (See v. 20.) Many of us would
say, "Quite easily." Rare is the Christian who hasn't run across
fellow believers with whom he does not agree, who do things he
does not like, and who are, in general, quite unlovable. But
John's words are plain: Christians are commanded to love God
and their brothers (see v. 21).

What John is saying in his usual black-and-white style is that,
for the Christian, loving your brother is not an option, it is an
opportunity and you do it out of obedience. If you are carrying a
grudge, treating your Christian brother indifferently (or looking
down on him with disdain as the Gnostics did), you are a liar.

John could have easily added the word *hypocrite*. The Greek
word for hypocrite suggests one who is playacting—wearing a
mask. It is all too easy to come to church, sing hymns about love
and grace, repeat the Lord's Prayer and then leave by another
door because you don't want to see so and so whom you have
not spoken to in weeks, months, and in some cases, years!

In Bruce Larson's candid words:

The hardest job of all is to love the people in the

household of God. It's much easier to seek out some
stranger in the street, to find some poor soul in need
and take him home for a night or two, or give him
some money, or pray with him. How about that person who has been sitting in the pew next to you or in
front of you for the last thirty years, with whom you
seem always to be at cross-purposes?[9]

For the imperfect Christian who sincerely seeks God's will,
but who knows frequent failure and weakness, John's "love or be
a liar" standard hits hard. What of those—particularly within the
Body of Christ—whom we honestly do not like or at least those
who have many characteristics and mannerisms we find unlikable? Is it honest or phony to admit, "I don't like him but I am
trying to love him"? And what about all those devotional books
or sermons that tell us, "Only Christians are capable of real
love"?

And there are still other problems. If Christians are the sole
possessors of "real" love, why do people in other faiths, even
members of certain well-known cults, display more love than we
do in our own churches? Why are Christians cynically described
as those who "shoot their wounded"? And why do people with
no particular faith of any kind sometimes appear more capable of
articulating and showing love for their fellowmen than those who
claim belief in Christ?

These are hard questions with no easy answers. They can
even be called unfair questions because they sound like a blanket
indictment of all Christians. They also make it sound like many
humanists, cultists and members of non-Christian faiths are
doing a great job of loving while Christians are failing left and
right. John's "black or white" tone adds to our discomfort. He
sounds like he is saying quite clearly that real Christians (true
believers) are commanded to love God and others, and if they do
not do so they are living a lie. If we want to play on the Christian
team, we are required to love, no exceptions, no time outs. But
what happens when we fail? Does John want us to turn in our
uniforms?

## Another look at three kinds of love

To try to sort it all out we need to go back to the three kinds of love discussed earlier: *eros, agape* and *phileo.* We find no real help in *eros,* which is self-centered and interested only in its own efforts to reach its personal goals. *Eros* can provide momentary enjoyment—even ecstacy—but it has nothing to do with learning how to love God and your brothers. It is no accident that *eros* does not appear even once in the New Testament.

In *phileo* we have more to work with. Phileo and its compounds appears nearly 100 times in the New Testament. Its most common use is to refer to showing a tender affection.[10] Other common interpretations of *phileo* are "brotherly love" and "friendship love." In order to have friendship, however, it takes two to do the loving. As Michael Harper says, "Friendship is founded on mutual liking—it is by nature reciprocal."[11]

With *agape* love we raise the entire discussion to a different level. Here we deal with an "unnatural" love that we are not capable of generating in our own strength. *Agape* doesn't bubble up out of our own hearts. Agape is an act of the will as we actively seek to obey God's command to love with no expectations or demands for any love in return.

*Agape* could be called "100-percent love"—unconditional, nothing held back, interested completely in the good of the one loved. *Phileo,* fine and noble as it can be, is not 100-percent love. Its reciprocal nature—giving but expecting to take something in return—leaves *phileo* at a different level.

British scholar W. E. Vine, who devoted his lifetime to exposition based on the original languages of the Bible, observes that *phileo* is never used in scriptural commands to love God. When Jesus laid down the two great commandments about loving God, and our neighbors as ourselves, the Greek verb is *agapeo.* When John speaks of God's command, "Whoever loves God must also love his brother" (v. 21), the verb again is *agapeo.*

To get a graphic picture of the difference between *phileo* love and *agape* love, we need only to flash back to that scene on the beach after Jesus' resurrection (see John 21:15-17). On the night before the crucifixion, Peter had vowed that he would never desert his Lord, but as Jesus had so clearly predicted,

Peter denied Him three times before the cock crowed. Now Jesus is confronting Peter on the beach and in keeping with his three denials He gives him three opportunities to answer the question: "Do you love me?"

In His first two questions, Jesus uses the word *agapeo* for love, suggesting that He is asking Peter for unselfish love—the kind that is ready to serve, with no expectation of love in return. But to those first two questions Peter answers with *phileo*— "Lord, you know I love you"—which is his honest admittal that he holds his Lord in highest esteem and affection but can claim no more than that at the moment.

In his third question, Jesus takes off the pressure a bit and also uses *phileo* when He asks, "Do you love me?" Again, Peter replies in kind, a bit hurt that the Lord would ask him still a third time (perhaps he is painfully reminded of his three denials at this moment).

As John records this incident in his Gospel, it can be no accident that he uses *phileo* and *agapeo* in this sequence. *Agape* love lies in the future for Peter (as well as all the disciples). *Agape* will come after Pentecost when they are empowered by the Holy Spirit. And Peter will learn more of *agape* when he has his vision on Cornelius's roof and learns that Gentiles are as welcome as Jews in God's Kingdom (see Acts 10:9-23).

The *agape* love John talks about here at the end of the fourth chapter is God's command for all Christians. In his comprehensive article on the topic of "love" in the *Zondervan Pictorial Encyclopedia of the Bible,* J. B. Funderburk points out that you cannot command someone to love in an emotional or feeling sense. *Phileo* is feeling love. *Phileo* involves warm feelings of affection and camaraderie—just plain liking to be with someone. *Agape* love, however, is a choice. The warm feelings of affection may not be there at all. That's why Jesus commanded His disciples to love their enemies with *agape* love and that is why John writes here in his letter that believers are to love one another with *agape* love because it is Christ's command, not an option they will exercise because they think somebody is intelligent enough, attractive enough, warm enough, or just plain pleasant to be around enough to deserve their love.[12]

**How do I *agapeo* thee?**

Greek word studies are interesting but we are still left grappling with just how we are to obey the command that John so clearly outlines for us. We understand love in terms of *eros* (sex, romance) and *phileo* (friendship, tender affection, really liking somebody). But when we speak of love as a choice, as an act of total sacrifice, we find ourselves groping for some kind of handle. Loving others when there is tension, disagreement, frustration, anger, etc., is perhaps the hardest work on the face of the earth.

In the winter of 1969 a coed at the University of Southern California committed suicide. She had been intelligent, witty, sensitive, with apparently everything to live for. One of her professors, Leo Buscaglia, pondered her death and wondered if there had been something he had missed, something he could have done to help prevent such a tragedy. Buscaglia's concern led to the establishment of a new class at U.S.C., which he simply called the "Love Class," taught on the professor's own time, with no offering of credit. Responses from his colleagues included everything from jeers and leers to charges of "irrelevant!"

Buscaglia, who refused to be discouraged, offered the class anyway. It was soon packed with more than 100 students. So hungry were people for anything resembling "real love," Buscaglia began speaking and writing on the subject. Several of his books became best-sellers including *Loving Each Other,* which was based on his survey of 600 people, ages 30 to 60 (two-thirds of whom were women).

The basic question Buscaglia asked all respondents was to list in order of importance three qualities that would build a loving relationship and three qualities that would destroy a relationship. The 10 most-named qualities for building love, in order of preference, discovered in Buscaglia's survey included: communication, affection, compassion/forgiveness, honesty, acceptance, dependability, sense of humor, romance (including sex), patience and freedom.

The 10 most-named qualities destructive to a relationship, in order of choice, were: lack of communication, selfishness/

unforgiving, dishonesty, jealousy, lack of trust, perfectionism, lack of flexibility (not open to change), lack of understanding, lack of respect, apathy.

*Loving Each Other* is essentially a discussion of the 10 constructive qualities Buscaglia found named in his survey. He sees these 10 qualities as skills that people need to learn, skills he believes are "as delicate . . . as those of the surgeon, the master builder and the gourmet cook."[13]

How does Buscaglia's list of things that build or destroy love help us learn how to show *agape* to those in the Body of Christ? After all, Buscaglia conducted his survey in a test group that was generally "run of the world" folk. All faiths and philosophical viewpoints were represented. But what if a similar survey was conducted among 600 Christians (or even 600,000)? Would the choices of constructive and destructive forces in a relationship be much different? For that matter, is Paul's list of what makes a loving relationship in 1 Corinthians 13 that much different? Paul speaks of patience, kindness, honesty, perseverance. He also speaks of what love is *not*: jealous, boastful, proud, rude, self-seeking, angry, grudge-holding.

In one sense, Scripture describes *agape* love as something to be learned in the same way a surgeon learns his craft. In a deeper sense, however, we see *agape* as something originating with God. That has been John's point through most of this fourth chapter. God is love. We can love only because God loved us first. The Holy Spirit has come to anoint and dwell in us. As we have seen, nothing happens in the Christian's life without the Holy Spirit (4:13-16).

Why then is *agape* love so hard? Because we do not let the Spirit work. John has given us Christ's command to love. We have our target and the ideal toward which we should grow. We can choose to grow or we can choose to shrink and become atrophied. We never stay the same.

Instead of waiting for God to zap us with an extra jolt of *agape* and suddenly "make us love somebody," we can choose to reach out to that somebody by trying to communicate, trying to be patient, trying to understand, trying to be honest, etc., etc. Whether you want to use Leo Buscaglia's list or Paul the apostle's, the principles are a great deal alike.

The crucial questions are: Am I willing to be available? Available to help? Available to be rejected? Can I disagree with someone, even have that person reject me, and still be available to help that person if I can ?

Once again we see that, on the surface, John's black-and-white words can sound threatening, even discouraging, but a little deeper look shows that the last thing he wants to do is discourage the sincere believer. He has told us God is perfecting His love is us (see 4:12). And now he has told us how we can perfect our love for Him. He is not saying we have to be perfect—score a 10 on every encounter we have throughout the day—but he has set up our target. It is not a question of "never missing the target or else." It is a matter of growth toward maturity and as we love our brother we "perfect" (complete) our love for God.

## Test Your Faith

Answering the following questions will help you better understand how you relate to others:

1. In your opinion, what is the one thing a Christian needs to fear? (See 1 John 4:18.)

2. This chapter discusses several qualities or conditions for building a loving relationship, including:

| | | |
|---|---|---|
| —communication | —affection | —compassion/ forgiveness |
| —acceptance | —dependability | —sense of humor |
| —honesty | —patience | —freedom |

Which of these qualities or conditions are clearly displayed in your church or Christian support group? Think of specific examples.

3. This chapter also discusses problems that erode or destroy relationships, including:

| | | |
|---|---|---|
| —lack of communication | —perfectionism | —unopen to change |
| —lack of respect | —lack of trust | —dishonesty |
| —lack of understanding | —lack of forgiveness | —apathy |
| —selfishness | | |

Which of the above are limiting or harming your church or Christian support group? What can you do about it?

4. Which of the following is the correct definition of *agape* love:
   a. Tender affection—brotherly love
   b. An act of the will as you actively seek to obey God's command to love with no exceptions or demands for any love in return
   c. Self-centered and interested only in its efforts to reach its personal goals.

5. If *agape* love comes from God, and all Christians have the Holy Spirit dwelling within them, why then is *agape* love still so difficult to demonstrate?

6. When is it hardest for you to display *agape* love? Who is involved? What usually happens? How could you pray to change this?

---

**Notes**

1. James Montgomery Boice, *The Epistles of John* (Grand Rapids: Zondervan Publishing House, 1979), p. 149.
2. 1 John 4:19.
3. For excellent insights on how much Nicodemus may have understood about "being born again," see William Barclay, *The Gospel of John,* vol. 1, Daily Study Bible (Edinburgh: The St. Andrew Press, 1955), pp. 113-116.

4. Many scholars believe that the Holy Spirit is the predominant idea throughout this section of John's letter. See, for example, John Stott, *The Epistles of John* (Grand Rapids: Wm. B. Eerdmans Publishing Co., 1960), pp. 165,166.

5. Calvin Miller, *The Song* (Downers Grove, IL: Inter-Varsity Press, 1977), p. 38.

6. Many commentators stress a major difference between John's two references to "perfected love" in chapter 4 of his letter. In 4:12 John is talking about how God perfects or completes His love in us. In 4:17 John is speaking of how we are to perfect or complete our love for God. The wording of the *NIV* translation of 4:17 is unfortunate because it deletes the Greek term, *en touto,* which means "herein" or "in this." In 4:16, John completes his description of how God is love and how He perfects His love in us through the indwelling Holy Spirit. As he moves into verse 17, what John intends to say is, "herein" or "because of all this—all that I have just told about God's love for you, your love for God can grow more and more." For an exhaustive discussion of the Greek term *en touto* in verse 17, see Robert L. Thomas, *Exegetical Digest of 1 John* (Robert L. Thomas, 1984), pp. 383-386.

7. Quoted in the *Encyclopedia of Religious Quotations,* Frank S. Mead ed. and comp. (Old Tappan, NJ: Fleming H. Revell Co., 1985), p. 144.

8. Michael Harper, *The Love Affair* (Grand Rapids: Wm. B. Eerdmans Publishing Co., 1982), pp. 70, 71.

9. Bruce Larson, *Wind and Fire* (Waco, TX: Word, Inc., 1984), p. 39.

10. W. E. Vine, *Vine's Expository Dictionary of Old and New Testament Words* (Old Tappan, NJ: Fleming H. Revell Co., 1981), vol. 2, p. 21.

11. Harper, *The Love Affair,* p. 58.

12. In the *Zondervan Pictorial Encyclopedia of the Bible,* vol. 3, J. B. Funderburk observes that you will find overlapping instances of the use of *phileo* and *agape* in Scripture. In other words, in some instances they seem to be used interchangeably. He still holds, however, that the basic difference is maintained (see for example, John 14:23; 16:27). The best distinction writes Funderburk is in the application of the two words. You cannot command *phileo*—it is either there or it is not. You cannot order people to be friends. But God does command *agape*—the Christians' clear choice to love someone regardless of how unlovable they are or how little they love in return. See. J. B. Funderburk, "Love," in *Zondervan Pictorial Encyclopedia,* Merrill C. Tenney and Steven Barabas eds. (Grand Rapids: Zondervan Publishing House, 1975), p. 990.

12. Leo Buscaglia, *Loving Each Other* (Thorofare, NJ: SLACK, Inc., 1984), p. 18.

# 13
## How to Be Sure You're Really Sure

*God steps in. Unannounced, He bursts into the soul, bringing forgiveness, cleansing, peace, a whole new perspective and dimension. He calls it "eternal life."*[1]
—*Chuck Swindoll*

*God has given us eternal life, and this life is in his Son. He who has the Son has life; he who does not have the Son of God does not have life.*[2]
—*The Apostle John*

I know I'm saved, but why do I have these thoughts?"

"I've been a faithful church member for years. Christ is my Saviour—but heaven? I hope so . . . "

"No one can be absolutely sure he's saved. Didn't Jesus say Himself that He's going to tell a lot of so-called believers, 'away from me—I never knew you'?"

Unfortunately, these are not mere hypothetical questions that make interesting discussion at lunch. They are all too real and too frequent among Christians now in our own day and Christians then in A.D. 90 when John wrote his Epistles. Is there any way to be absolutely sure of our salvation? As John moves into his concluding paragraphs he focuses on this question more closely than ever:

### 1 John 5:1-5

Everyone who believes that Jesus is the Christ is born of God, and everyone who loves the father loves his child as well. This is how we know that we love the children of God: by loving God and carrying out his commands. This is love for God: to obey his commands. And his commands are not burdensome, for everyone born of God has overcome the world. This is the victory that has overcome the world, even our faith. Who is it that overcomes the world? Only he who believes that Jesus is the Son of God.

Throughout his letter, John presents test after test to assure the true Christians and strike fear in the hearts of the heretics. As he opens chapter 5 he fires one more round of ideas built upon his three basic questions:

- "Do you believe?"
- "Do you obey?"
- "Do you love?"

Obviously the Gnostics would fail miserably on all three counts. They did not believe Jesus was truly God incarnate. They did not obey God's moral teachings, and they made light of sin. They did not love, but taught instead a form of elitist pride and divisiveness that really boiled down to hatred for those who were not "spiritually enlightened."

## Love is obedience, not warm fuzzies

In the first three verses of chapter 5, John braids love, belief and obedience into a strong cord that binds the Christian tightly to Christ. All three concepts are the result of God's loving and active work in the life of the believer.

In 5:1 and 2 John is saying the same thing he said in 4:19: We can believe, love and obey because God first loved us (begat us as His children). In 5:3 John nicely sums up the heart and soul of *agape* love. We can love God and others—through obedience, not warm fuzzy feelings. And this kind of obedience is not done with clenched teeth and resentment. As we learn to love with *agape* we are responding to God's *agape*. God commands us to love; our loving response to Him makes it possible to obey. God's commands are not nit-picking, legalistic burdens like those of the Pharisees (see Matt. 23:1-7). As God Himself (the Son) said, "My yoke is easy and my burden is light" (Matt. 11:30).

## How to always be a winner

In 1 John 5:4 and 5 John's thoughts flow on to possibly the most encouraging lines of his entire letter. Everyone born of God—those who believe that Jesus is God's incarnate Son—are always winners in the battle against the pagan system called the world. The Christian's secret weapon is faith. Commentators differ on what John means when he says our faith has overcome the world (see v. 4). He may be talking about the initial victory of the Christian when he believes and is converted. He may be talking about various occasions when the Christian conquers temptation. Or, he may be referring to victories won over the

Gnostic heretics, who had left the Church because their teachings were rejected. (See also John's other references to victories over the counterfeit teachings of the Gnostics in 2:19 and 4:4.)

In verse 5, however, John switches from past tense and talks about what God is *still doing* through our faith. We overcome the world as we continue to believe and trust in Jesus as the Son of God. Through our faith we continue to win victories over the pressures of a godless secular society that entices us with the lust of the flesh, the lust of the eyes and the pride of life (see 2:16).

"Who is it that overcomes the world?" asks John. He answers that only the one who believes in Jesus as the Son of God can overcome the world. John is strongly underlining a basic Christian principle: There is no victory over the world except through Christ. Faith in Christ is the secret to "always being a winner."

"Sounds simple enough," we say, and under our breath we add, "but why are so many Christians being defeated? Why the stampede to the beach on Sunday morning instead of to church? Why all the divorces among Christians? Why all the unwed Christian mothers?"

Yes, why? John's answer is still the same. The key to winning is to have faith—to trust God fully and completely, not just enough to feel saved while you go on with a life-style that capitulates to the world instead of to the lordship of Jesus Christ.

## The sexual tidal wave rolls on

And no more obvious example of capitulation can currently be found than sex and the "new morality" that has swept over society like a tsunami tidal wave rolls over a Pacific atoll. It is quite common to see a "Christian" couple approach a pastor and announce they have been living together but want to get married. When the paster asks them to at least recognize their sin, repent and live apart until the day of the marriage, they leave in a huff, complaining about the pastor's "lack of love and understanding."Besides, doesn't he realize it's a lot cheaper to live together?

In *Flirting with the World,* John White laments the deterioration of sexual mores which has taken place in little more than one generation. He writes:

> Literally, anything goes, except self-discipline, obedience to biblical principles, sexual abstinence before marriage, and faithfulness to one's marriage partner. Our young people are exposed to a society that countenances unparalleled promiscuity, and to churches so out of touch with the relevant Scriptures and so spiritually bankrupt that they are ripe for Satan's plucking.[3]

White goes on to relate his attempt to counsel a 20-year-old Christian woman who shared that she had two boyfriends. Her "old" boyfriend, whom she had been dating some four years, was getting a bit dull, so she took up with a "new" boyfriend. Her new boyfriend, once known as "wild", was a new convert to Christ. The girl confessed that she intended to marry neither young man, but that she had "a lot of fun" engaging in mutual masturbation with the "old" boyfriend and oral sex with the "new" one. White concludes the anecdote by observing that this young woman is "typical of a large proportion of Christian young people today."[4]

Your reaction to the above story could be anything from total horror and judgment—"the girl *can't* be a real believer!" to a shrug—"I know several people living the same way." Whatever you want to call it, it is doubtful John would see it as "overcoming the world." But doesn't this young lady believe that Jesus is the Son of God? It is quite likely that she would say yes. Does she believe Jesus is her lord and master and that she should live to please Him? It is quite likely she would admit the answer is no.

Case closed. Or is it? Openly-promiscuous behavior is easy enough to judge. But what about: gossip, quietly lusting while watching provocative scenes on TV, practicing not-so-subtle racism as you share jokes with Christian friends? Does it make any difference where the problem lies? Is the gossip, the voyeur or the racist any more victorious over the world than the unmarried Christian girl who masturbates one boyfriend and has oral sex with the other?

John has the key to why so many Christians feel the agony of defeat instead of the thrill of victory over the world. He can tell us why we ask ourselves, "Will I really make it to heaven? Does this Christian life stuff actually *work*?"

Yes, it works—*if.* The *Living Bible* paraphrase of verses 4 and 5 of 1 John underscores that "if" in vivid language: "Every child of God can obey him, defeating sin and evil pleasure by trusting Christ to help him. But who could possibly fight and win this battle except by believing that Jesus is truly the Son of God?"

These verses contain one of those self-evident principles that we tend to overlook because it is so familiar: For the Christian, victory over sin in the world rides or falls with how we see Jesus Christ. If we call Him the "Son of God," do we grasp the full implications? Is being born again a nice neat transaction comparable to joining the Rotary or local women's club? As John continues, he assures us there is much more to it than that:

### 1 John 5:6-12

This is the one who came by water and blood—Jesus Christ. He did not come by water only, but by water and blood. And it is the Spirit who testifies, because the Spirit is the truth. For there are three that testify: the Spirit, the water and the blood; and the three are in agreement. We accept man's testimony, but God's testimony is greater because it is the testimony of God, which he has given about his Son. Anyone who believes in the Son of God has this testimony in his heart. Anyone who does not believe God has made him out to be a liar, because he has not believed the testimony God has given about his Son. And this is the testimony: God has given us eternal life, and this life is in his Son. He who has the Son has life; he who does not have the Son of God does not have life.

While John's main theme is always love, he seems to have a certain appreciation for legal matters. For the second time (see 2:1,2 for the first instance), John uses a courtroom analogy to make his point. In verses 6 to 8 of chapter 5 he speaks of three "witnesses" who testify concerning who Jesus Christ is and what He did: (1) water; (2) blood; (3) the Spirit. Scholars offer several possible interpretations of "water and blood," but the context in which John writes points to equating the water with Jesus' baptism and the blood with His death on the cross.[5]

The reason the context of John's reference to water and blood points most clearly to Jesus' baptism and death on the cross is John's battle with Gnostic heresy. The reason John sets up his "courtroom scene" and brings forth his witnesses is to prove his case for the deity of Jesus Christ one final and convincing time.

To confirm that Jesus is the incarnate Son of God, John goes back to the two most significant events of Jesus' life on earth: His baptism, in which God declared He was indeed His beloved Son as He bestowed on Him the Holy Spirit (Matt. 3:13-17); His death, in which He shed His blood for the sins of the entire world (1 John 2:2).

It is not by accident that John uses the words *Jesus Christ* in verse 6. He wants everyone to understand that there is no difference between Jesus and the Christ. They are inseparably linked. It is also no accident that John says Jesus came by water *and* blood. Here he is confronting head-on the most serious Gnostic heresy of them all: the denial that the death of Christ had any significance for sinful man.

You remember that Gnostic teachers like Cerinthus accepted the idea that the man Jesus was empowered by the "heavenly Christ" at His baptism in the Jordan River.

Gnostic teachers had no problem with giving lip service to Jesus' baptism, saying it was a means of temporarily empowering Him for His ministry. But they refused to grant any significance to Jesus' death. They refused to admit that Jesus the Christ had reconciled man to God by shedding His blood to cleanse him from sin (see 1 John 1:7; also Rom. 5:9; Heb. 9:14; 1 Pet. 1:18,19; and Rev. 1:5).

## The life blood of Christianity

What Jesus shed on the cross was far more than the plasma, corpuscles and platelets of a mere man. His was the very life blood of the Christian faith. One of the most important—and least understood—concepts in Scripture is the shedding of blood to obtain forgiveness of sins. Robert Coleman estimates there are 460 specific references to blood in the Bible. If we count related concepts such as altar, sacrifice, offering and atonement, Colemen doubts that there is a page in the Bible that does not allude to the blood in some way. "It is the scarlet thread that weaves the whole scope of revelation into one harmonious witness to the drama of redemption."[6]

With his Jewish background, John was well aware of the importance the Israelites placed on the shedding of blood to atone for sins. In fact, they climaxed each year with a special Day of Atonement (see Lev. 16:1-34; 23:17-32; Num. 29:7-11). Two bullocks and one goat were slain and their blood was sprinkled to atone for the sins of the priests and all the people.

But even this wasn't enough. A second goat was brought forward over which the high priest would confess the sins of all the people, just in case there was somebody present whose conscience was not clear or who had forgotten some sin he may have committed in ignorance or carelessness. This goat was then led away into the wilderness and released. From this practice we get our term *scapegoat*—someone who takes the blame for others.

As thorough as the Israelites were with their Day of Atonement rituals, all of these sacrifices never really removed sin. They could only cover it temporarily, and new sacrifices constantly had to be offered. When Christ, the Lamb of God, took away the sins of the world by dying on the cross (see John 1:29; 1 Cor. 5:7; 1 Pet. 1:19), further sacrifices were unnecessary.

## The Holy Spirit clinches John's case

To clinch his case, John calls his third witness, the Holy Spirit, who is the truth (see 1 John 5:6).

As John calls his third and most important witness to testify on behalf of Jesus as the Christ, he may be thinking of how the false witnesses could not agree when they testified against Jesus at His trial (see Mark 14:56-59). Jewish law stated: "A matter must be established by the testimony of two or three witnesses" (Deut. 19:15).

"If we can accept the testimony of three men," says John, "surely we can accept the greater threefold testimony of God." Obviously, John's "case" could be challenged in a human court of law. But John isn't trying this case in a human (worldly) court. In fact, he is trying the world (which includes the Gnostic heretics) in a spiritual court, so to speak, where the Holy Spirit is a powerful inner witness to all those who are born again—the very ones John is trying to convince and assure. If the witness of man stands up in a human court of law, surely, says John, the threefold witness of God, spearheaded by the Holy Spirit, will be even stronger in the heart of the Christian believer (see 1 John 2:27; 3:24; John 15:26; 16:13; 1 Cor. 2:9-16).

That is precisely what John means in verse 10 of 1 John 5 when he says: "The man who really believes in the Son of God will find God's testimony in his own heart" (*Phillips*).

For all believers who read his words, John has an open-and-shut case. The three witnesses—water, blood and the Spirit—win the day.

With the Gnostics, who do not believe in the incarnate Son, John "loses" the argument, but the Gnostic lose much more. By refusing to accept God's own testimony concerning His Son, they call God a liar. Is John being fair when he calls someone who does not believe a "liar"? In the case of the Gnostics, absolutely. The Gnostics had chosen to infiltrate the Christian faith and twist its doctrines to suit themselves. They were entitled to their opinions, to be sure, but not to spreading errors, lies, hatred and discord in the Church.

John writes primarily with the Gnostics in mind, but are they the only ones for whom his message is intended? Down through the centuries many have made the mistake of calling God a liar and therefore forfeited the gift of eternal life. John Robert Ingersol, brilliant agnostic and archenemy of Christianity, on his deathbed confessed: "Life is a narrow vale between the cold and barren peaks of two eternities. We strive in vain to look beyond the heights. We cry aloud, and the only answer is the echo of our wailing cry."[7]

John's main goal in this passage is to help Christian believers know that life is far more than a narrow vale between two cold and barren peaks. He wants all Christians to *be sure they are sure* of their salvation. First John 5:11 and 12 spells out "God's testimony" in crystal clear terms: God has given us eternal life through His Son. If you have the Son, you have life. Refuse the Son and you forfeit eternal life.

These are grim words of warning to those who refuse to believe; they are blessed words of assurance to those who doubt their salvation, or worry about their box score in the battle for victory over the world. The answer to doubts and worries is faith in Jesus Christ, an all-out, stake-my-eternal-life-on-it faith. You can't quite muster that much faith? It doesn't matter. As Francis Schaeffer says, it isn't your faith that saves you, it's the *object* of your faith. "Not feeling sure" is not the point. The Christian relies on the *fact* of Jesus Christ.

John can really say no more than he already has to Christians who may struggle with doubts or confusion. His three tests, repeated three times each, have examined every facet of what it means to obey, to love and to believe. If our doubts persist perhaps we have trapped ourselves by subconsciously editing those three questions to read:

- "Do I obey *enough*?"
- "Do I love *enough*?"
- "Do I believe *enough*?"

All these questions are the wrong questions because they all do the same thing. They keep imperfect believers like ourselves wondering if we have performed according to some impossible standard God is demanding that we must meet. The critical thing we must understand is that when John asks us if we obey, love and believe, his tests are not quantitative. It is not a question of "how much" we pass each test. The real question is our *willingness to take the tests*.

Indeed, if a Christian is doubting his salvation or victory over the world because he thinks he does not believe, obey or love enough, it is almost always true that this person *does* have eternal life in the Son. Without the new birth caused by God's seed being planted within, there would be no concern (see 1 John 3:9).

To put it another way, the questions a Christian should ask are these: Is my heart right? Have I been born again? Have I done business with God through His incarnate Son and no other?

Other questions follows, of course. For example:

- "Do I admit I am a sinner in need of God's saving grace?" (Eph. 2:8,9).
- "Do I repent, that is, do I want to turn from my sin and live for God, not Satan?" (Acts 3:19; 17:30).
- "Do I confess my sin, that is, do I agree with God that I am a sinner?" (Rom. 3:23).
- "Do I accept God's answer for my sin in the death and resurrection of Jesus Christ, who was God incarnate?" (1 Cor. 15:3,4).
- "Do I accept Christ as my Lord—the One I seek to obey and please in all that I do?" (Rom. 10:9,10; 1 Cor. 8:6).

It is on this last question that many believers stumble. John's black-and-white approach makes it difficult to live in the gray. Perhaps a lot of people doubt their salvation because deep down they resist admitting Christ as their Lord. The saviour part is no problem. Everybody needs a good fire insurance policy. But lordship? This can cramp one's style. God may start to meddle, to demand too much. After all, nobody's perfect.

But then, God isn't asking us to live "perfect" lives. He is asking us to live lives of faith and commitment. Go back to a question we asked earlier: Do we really understand the implications when we say we believe "that Jesus is the Son of God" (1 John 5:5)? There is far more involved here than simply "getting our doctrine straight." William Barclay said it well:

To believe in Jesus Christ is not simply to accept what He says is true; it is to commit all life into His

hands and into His direction; it is to place ourselves
in His hands in time and in eternity.[8]

## *Test Your Faith*

To help you "to be sure you're really sure," answer the following questions:

1. For me, obedience is:
   a. Impossible
   b. Difficult
   c. A constant battle
   d. Getting a little easier.
How would you explain the answer you chose?

2. For me, "overcoming the world" is:
   a. A nice theory
   b. A growing reality
   c. A worthy goal
   d. Difficult in certain areas.
How would you explain the answer you chose?

3. For me, the atonement is:
   a. An important doctrine
   b. The lifeblood of my faith
   c. How Christ took the blame for me
   d. Hard to understand.

4. Robert Ingersoll, the famous atheist, described life as "a narrow vale between the cold and barren peaks of two eternities."
How would you describe life?
   a. A wide-open plain leading to eternal life
   b. A bumpy road to heaven
   c. A confusing maze
   d. A road with a lot of detours.
How would you explain your definition?

5. I make Christ my Lord:
    a. Always
    b. More and more
    c. Sometimes
    d. Seldom.

At what point does Christ need to have more lordship in your life?

---

## Notes

1. Charles R. Swindoll, *Growing Strong in the Seasons of Life* (Portland: Multnomah Press, 1983), p. 118.
2. 1 John 5:11,12.
3. John White, *Flirting with the World* (Wheaton, IL: Harold Shaw Publishers, 1982), p. 75.
4. Ibid., p. 75.
5. Down through the centuries, several interpretations of "water and blood" in 1 John 5:6 have been held. Reformers like Luther and Calvin tied the words to the sacraments of baptism and the Lord's Supper. Church fathers like Augustine equated John's reference with the water and blood that came from Jesus' side on the cross after a Roman soldier thrust a spear into Him. For why these older interpretations do not hold up, see John Stott, *The Epistles of John* (Grand Rapids: Wm. B. Eerdmans Publishing Co., 1960), pp. 177, 178.
6. Robert Coleman, *The New Covenant* (Colorado Springs: NavPress Publishing Co., 1984), p. 10.
7. Quoted by Charles Swindoll, *Growing Strong in the Seasons of Life* p. 217.
8. William Barclay, *The Letters of John and Jude* The Daily Study Bible (Edinburgh: The St. Andrew Press, 1958), p. 133.

# 14
# P.S. He Loves You

*He who knows not, and knows that he knows not,*
*is a child; teach him.*
*He who knows, and knows not that he knows,*
*is asleep; wake him.*
*He who knows, and knows that he knows,*
*is wise; follow him.*
—*Persian Proverb*

*I write these things to you who believe in the*
*name of the Son of God so that you may*
*know that you have eternal life.*[1]
—*The Apostle John*

B ruce Larson tells of a story related to him by a professor from an Ivy League school. It seems the head of the astronomy department was trying to impress the head of the divinity school with his theological acumen.

"Now, let's face it," said the astronomy professor, "in religion, what it all boils down to very simply is that you should love your neighbor as yourself. It's the Golden Rule, right?"

"Yes, I suppose that's true," answered the divinity school dean. "Just as in astronomy it all boils down to one thing—'Twinkle, twinkle, little star.'"

The moral of this encounter, observes Larson, is our tendency to try to make truth so simple that it becomes ridiculous. Then we can brush it off as "not that important."[2]

As John pens his next statement, he boils down to one sentence his major reason for writing his letter, but he has a lot more on his mind than "Twinkle, twinkle, little star." John's one sentence spoke volumes of assurance to those who read it in A.D. 90, and it speaks volumes to those who read it today:

### 1 John 5:13
I write these things to you who believe in the name of the Son of God so that you may know that you have eternal life.

With verse 13, John begins what is called his "assurance postscript." Assurance is obviously the major subject of his concluding remarks. He wants his readers to be sure they *know* God really does love them. To make sure, he uses the word know seven times in verses 13 to 21. In all but one place he uses the Greek word *oida*[3] which refers to "fullness of knowledge"— that is, something considered an absolute fact (see vv. 13, 15 twice, 18, 19 and 20). In the seventh instance, John switches to the Greek term *ginosko,* for reasons we will examine later.

Not surprisingly, John leads off with his most important assurance for all believers: To believe in the Son of God is to *know you have eternal life*. First John 5:13 is an echo of John's gospel (20:31) where John said: "But these are written that you may believe that Jesus is the Christ, the Son of God, and that by believing you might have life in his name."

While John 20:31 and 1 John 5:13 are similar, there is one distinct difference. In John 20:31 the apostle writes to help people believe that Jesus is the Christ and thereby acquire eternal life. In 1 John 5:13, John writes to assure readers who already believe that they indeed have eternal life. It seems likely that John wrote his Gospel first, for evangelistic purposes, and then followed up with his Epistle as sort of a "covering letter" to instruct and guide believers.[4] With assurance of eternal life serving as his cornerstone (see v. 13), John continues to build his fortress of certainties for Christians. His next section could be called "The Foundation of Answered Prayer":

### 1 John 5:14-17

This is the assurance we have in approaching God: that if we ask anything according to his will, he hears us. And if we know that he hears us— whatever we ask—we know that we have what we asked of him.

If anyone sees his brother commit a sin that does not lead to death, he should pray and God will give him life. I refer to those whose sin does not lead to death. There is a sin that leads to death. I am not saying that he should pray about that. All wrongdoing is sin, and there is sin that does not lead to death.

## Can we simply "name it and claim it"?

There are many assurances and promises in Scripture regarding prayer. For example:

- Mark 11:24: "Therefore I tell you, whatever you ask for in prayer, believe that you have received it, and it will be yours."

- Luke 11:9: "So I say to you: Ask and it will be given to you; seek and you will find; knock and the door will be opened to you."
- John 16:24: "Until now you have not asked for anything in my name. Ask and you will receive, and your joy will be complete."

Verses like the above can be lifted out of context and made to sound as if God is giving Christians *carte blanche* to "name it and claim it." But as John ends his letter, he balances the scale, so to speak, by laying down the key principle of all prayer: Whatever we ask must be according to God's will.

In 5:14, 15, John sends us good news and bad news. The good news is that we can pray with "boldness toward God," which is the literal meaning of *parresia* (translated "assurance" in the *NIV* and "confidence" in the *NASB* and *KJV*). Furthermore, if we can be sure God hears us, we can be sure we will receive what we request.

The bad news centers on that little word *if.* For any number of reasons, it's possible our prayers won't be according to God's will. We are left walking that old tightrope called, "How can I really know God's will in *this* situation?"

And there is still another problem. Tacking "if it be your will, Lord" on our prayers can become a cop-out. The "copping-out" enters in when our faith is weak and we doubt that God can or will answer our prayer. We put in a qualifier that sounds spiritual, but at the same time we won't be embarrassed or disappointed when God "doesn't come through."

## Some guidelines for praying in God's will

Until we achieve omniscience (become as all-knowing as God Himself), there is no absolute fail-safe way to know that we are always praying according to God's will There are, however, some excellent guidelines to follow:

> *One.* Is my request in line with what God has revealed in Christ and the Scriptures? In other

words, am I trying to glorify God or myself?

*Two.* If God grants my request, will it draw me closer to Him? As John spelled out in his "God is love" discourse (1 John 4:7-21), will God's love be perfected (completed) in me and will I take another step in perfecting (completing) my love for Him and others?

*Three.* Will granting my request be the best thing for everyone? That is, am I being concerned with the bigger picture or only with my little portion?

*Four.* In making this request am I seeking first the Kingdom of God? Can both God and I enjoy the results?[5]

As for copping-out by saying "if it be your will, Lord," the real question is how much you really want God's will and not your own. As author and scholar William Barclay puts it: "We are so apt to think that prayer is asking God for what we want, whereas true prayer is asking God for what He wants."[6]

The best way to avoid cop-out prayers is to take some advice John gave way back in chapter 2, verse 6: Whoever claims to live in him must walk as Jesus did. Entire libraries have been written on what it means to walk as Jesus walked. Whatever these phrases mean, they have to include the willingness to accept whatever God has for us—to want what He wants. It follows then, as day follows night, that we will want to pray "according to his will."

Suppose, then, we have done our best to follow guidelines like those listed above and that we are sincerely trying to walk as Jesus did. According to John's line of reasoning in 5:14 and 15, it should all work like this:

*One.* We can have bold assurance as we approach God in prayer, if we ask according to His will.

*Two.* When we ask according to His will, we know He hears us.

*Three.* And because we know He hears us, we know we will receive what we have requested.

Does this mean God will always grant every prayer "on the spot"? Anyone who has been a Christian for more than an hour or two knows this isn't how it works. A key element in prayer is patience. The answer may eventually be yes; it may eventually be no; it is often "Wait." One reason God may delay His answer is that we aren't quite ready for it. If God did answer our prayer, there might be a price we wouldn't be ready to pay. As Augustine is supposed to have put it: "Oh God, make me pure, but not right away."[7]

In the classic book on prayer, *The Kneeling Christian,* the Unknown Author recalls the experience of George Müller, who may have had more prayers answered in his lifetime of caring for orphans then any person who ever lived. Müller prayed for 63 years and eight months for a certain friend's conversion. Said Müller late in life, "He is not converted yet, but he will be! How can it be otherwise? There is the unchanging promise of Jehovah, and on that I rest."

Müller died with his friend unconverted, but that same friend came to Christ before George Müller was laid in his grave![8]

## Solving the puzzle of prayer

In 1 John 5:14 and 15, we have a tremendous promise that is also a puzzle. We are always to pray according to God's will, but at the same time we are instructed to ask for what we need, believing it will be given.

The Reverend W. L. Vaswig observes that any real relationship with true communication has a certain element of struggle and risk. One of the best illustrations is Jesus' relationship to His Father. In the Garden of Gethsemane He struggled in agony asking the Father to take the cup of horrible pain from Him. *Then* He prayed, "Not my will but yours be done." Vaswig writes:

> It is precisely because we have an intimate relationship with God that we are able to pray asking for "whatever." We do not disregard the question of God's will. But because we know God, and he knows us, we are able to "know" in prayer how God will

respond. In petitionary prayer, we know God so intimately that the answer to the prayer is in our hearts
even before the request is made. It is much like a
good marriage relationship. After thirty-one years
with Marcine I know ahead of time, in most cases,
how she will respond to a given request or idea. As
time goes by and new situations come up, we get to
know each [other] better and better. So it is in our
walk with God.[9]

The better we know God the more 1 John 5:14 and 15 will
mean in our lives. Is what we are asking always God's will?
Sometimes we just don't know. Sometimes there just isn't
enough time to go through guidelines that ask profound questions like, "Will this advance your Kingdom, Lord?" Sometimes,
to paraphrase Luther's words, we will simply have to pray boldly
and trust God to hear our childish petitions.

Perhaps what John is trying to tell us is that honestly wanting
God's will in all things removes all the pressure when we pray.
We know He will answer. Whatever the answer is, we "have
what we have asked of Him" because our asking is unshakably
rooted in wanting what *He* wants.

## Who might commit the sin unto death?

In 5:16 and 17, John switches the subject to intercessory
prayer. His advice on praying for others has puzzled many commentators over the centuries. What John seems to do is separate sin into two categories: sins that lead to death and sins that
do not. We should pray for the brethren we see committing the
"lesser" sins, but for those committing the "greater" sins—the
sins leading to death—John is not as insistent. He doesn't give a
firm yes or a firm no on praying for them. He simply says, "I am
not saying that he should pray about that" (v. 16). The gist of
what he is saying is that when the "sin that leads to death" is
involved, there is no assurance our prayers will be that effective.[10]

What did John mean by "the sin that leads to death"? Some of
the early Christian fathers thought he spoke of specific "unfor-

givable" sins like murder and adultery. Other theories offered
over the years describe the unforgivable sin as apostasy
(renouncing the faith) or blasphemy against the Holy Spirit. The
Pharisees were guilty of blasphemy against the Holy Spirit when
they rejected the miracles of Jesus and claimed He was doing the
work of the devil, not the Holy Spirit (Mark 3:20-30).

Whatever John has in mind, the Gnostics and their heretical
teachings have to be part of his thinking. If anyone had rejected
the work of the Holy Spirit through Jesus Christ it was the Gnostic teachers who were masquerading as fountains of valid Christian theology. John has already referred to the Gnostics as "little
antichrists" (see 2:18-23), "children of the devil" (3:10), and
"false prophets" (4:1-6). But here he makes the most serious
charge of all. The Gnostics had committed the sin that leads to
death by thoroughly and completely and finally rejecting Jesus
Christ. John's words are a sobering reminder that it is possible
to put yourself beyond the reach of God's grace, and that sin is
never "trivial," because all sin has the potential for leading to
death and spiritual ruin.[11]

John's "fortress of faith" is starting to take shape. So far he
has laid the cornerstone (assurance of eternal life, 5:13), and the
foundation (assurance of answered prayer, 5:14-17). Now we
will see John add four walls of further certainties to the fortress
in which any Christian can dwell in confidence and safety. He
describes three of those walls in his next paragraph:

### 1 John 5:18-20
We know that anyone born of God does not continue
to sin; the one who was born of God keeps him safe,
and the evil one does not touch him. We now that we
are children of God, and that the whole world is
under the control of the evil one. We know also that
the Son of God has come and has given us understanding, so that we may know him who is true. And
we are in him who is true—even in his Son Jesus
Christ. He is the true God and eternal life.

The first wall of certainty in faith's fortress reinforces the same truth John introduced in chapter 3: If you are born again you *know* you cannot continue to sin (compare 3:6,9 to 5:18). A Christian isn't perfect, but he does have an aversion to sin. To be born again is to be at war with sin, with no possibility of truce or armistice.

Not only are we at war with sin, but we are winning! We are kept from Satan's touch (actually, "grasp" is a better meaning in the Greek). And who keeps us? Jesus Christ, God's only begotten Son. "We know that the true child of God does not sin (habitually and without concern or conviction), he is in the charge of God's own Son and the evil one cannot touch him" (1 John 5:18, *Phillips*).

## We have met the enemy and guess what?

But wait. How do we explain the obvious (and all too frequent) instances when a Christian does slip into sin? What about certain sinful hang-ups and attitudes that plague us? Is John being realistic here or is this the idealism of a loving old man who is out of touch with "real life"?

We get a major clue in verse 19, the second wall of our fortress. Here John compares the state of a Christian to the condition of the world. The Christian *knows* he is God's child (under His care and control) while the world (the godless system of pagan men) is under Satan's control. The Greek expression here suggests that the world does not struggle or writhe in Satan's grasp; instead it lies quietly, practically asleep.[12]

John's words are strong and brutally frank. For John there are always only two conditions: You can belong to Christ or belong to the world. You can be under God's rule or under the world rulers of this present darkness (see Eph. 6:12).[13]

With whom or what, then, does a Christian struggle when he all too frequently seems to slip and slide on those banana peels we call sins? Pogo, the well-loved cartoon character, knew the answer: "We have met the enemy and he is *us!*" Our primary struggle is with the flesh (our sinful human nature). James describes the familiar cycle: Our desire (the flesh) entices us, conceives and gives birth to sin (Jas. 1:14,15). Obviously, we need to practice spiritual birth control—but how?

We get an excellent clue in a story about Adolph Ochs, who published the *New York Times* in the 1920s. Business was bad and Ochs was known to save a few cents on the electric bill by wandering through the newspaper offices late at night turning off lights. Then a trusted friend offered him a $150,000 advertising contract, "No strings attached." But Ochs refused! Why? He was afraid he would be so dependent on such a huge account he would be tempted to compromise the newspaper's integrity in order to keep the advertising money coming in![14]

Adolph Och's example has much to teach the Christian who struggles with "besetting sins." Often our problem is that we wait until we are beset by the sin and then we try to find a way to resist. By then, of course, it's too late. Desire conceives, sin is born and we lose another round. True, we have the way out through confession and being forgiven through Christ's atonement (see 1 John 1:9–2:2). But, how much more growth, joy and satisfaction there can be in nipping sin in the bud before it can defeat us. Imperfect as we are, we can't win them all, but we can win a lot more often!

## Getting to know Him better and better

John goes on to build the third wall of our fortress of faith by emphasizing what we know through Jesus Christ. In verse 20, John uses two Greek terms for the word *know*. First he says we know (*oida*—absolute fact) Christ the Son has come and given us an understanding. What kind of understanding? The kind that helps us know (*ginosko*) God better and better.

The Greek term *ginosko* suggests progressing in knowledge, growing toward complete understanding. W. E. Vine observes that in the New Testament the Greek term *ginosko* frequently indicates a relationship.[15] What John is saying here is this: Because we have our doctrine (the absolute facts) straight about Jesus Christ, we have the privilege of building a relationship with God through Him. As we go back to read 5:18-20 in one breath, we see three walls of our fortress of faith joining solidly together:

*One*. We know we can conquer sin (v. 18) because . . .

*Two.* We are God's children (v. 19) and . . .
*Three.* We have increasing knowledge of the only
true God (v. 20).

First John 5:18 to 20 could be called the Christian's Excedrin
passage. The next time life's headaches start pounding on your
Christian assurance and confidence, take these three verses to
heart, then call God in the morning to say, "Amen" and "Thank
You"!

One more wall of our fortress of faith remains to be erected.
In his parting word, however, John does not use a certainty.
Instead, he chooses an admonition:

## 1 John 5:21

Dear children, keep yourselves from idols.

At first glance, verse 21 seems like an abrupt—even odd—
way for John to end his letter. Was he in a hurry to make the
next courier headed for the outlying towns around Ephesus? If
he had taken more time would he have rearranged some paragraphs and closed the Epistle with a more "logical" thought,
such as verse 13: "I write these things to you who believe in the
name of the Son of God so that you may know that you have
eternal life"?

One answer to this kind of speculation is that the letter of 1
John is in the form in which John wrote it while under the inspiration of the Holy Spirit (see 2 Tim. 3:16; 2 Pet. 1:21). One does
not "edit" the Holy Spirit.

But there is an even better answer. Throughout his letter,
John has had two major concerns: (1) to assure Christians of
who they are and what they have in Jesus Christ; (2) to warn
them against idolatry—putting some other belief, practice or
attitude ahead of God's truth, which is found in His Son, Jesus
Christ.

John knew that the very existence of the Christian faith was
at stake, because false teachers were undermining and destroy-

ing its unique foundation—the incarnation of God in Jesus Christ. The incarnation puts Christianity above and beyond any religious or philosophical system before (or since). To accept anything less than God incarnate in the Son is to practice idolatry.

## Selfism: the ultimate idolatry

Perhaps John chose to end his letter with this cryptic warning because he knew how idolatrous we really are. We make idols out of just about anything. We idolize beauty, youth, talent and success. We idolize possessions, property, prestige and power. We idolize pleasure, leisure, learning and our independence. We even idolize health.

Above all, we idolize ourselves.

Professor Paul Vitz describes this ultimate idolatry as *selfism*: being preoccupied with your own ego and personal fulfillment.[16] We live in the day of "I gotta be me!" and "I'll do it *my* way." Plagued by lack of self-esteem, we substitute self-indulgence for self-acceptance and self-importance for genuine self-worth.

In *Flirting with the World,* psychiatrist John White laments the confusion in the Christian community over passages like: "Love your neighbor as yourself." Many of us are prone to think, "Surely, this is an argument for having high self-esteem. How can I love my neighbor properly if I don't love myself first?" White wonders, however, if high self-esteem is automatically the opposite of low self-esteem. He points to verses like Romans 12:3, which tells us not to think of ourselves more highly than we ought to think (see also Phil. 2:3,4). White believes a better term for self-esteem is "realistic self-appraisal." In other words, instead of seeking high self-esteem, we should seek self-acceptance through our knowledge of knowing that God has accepted us.[17]

When Christ called "love your neighbor as yourself" the second Great Commandment (see Matt. 22:39; Lev. 19:18), He was describing how we are to act toward our neighbor, not how we are to feel about our psyche. To love one's neighbor as one's self is to reach out to help others in whatever way possible. John taught the same truth back in 1 John 3:16 to 18. We are to share what we have with our brothers. We are not to love simply with words and tongue but with actions and in truth. A little later in his letter, John taught us that because God loved us enough to send His Son to be an atoning sacrifice for sins, we *ought* to love one another (4:10,11).

John also echoes Jesus when he says, "We love because he first loved us" (4:19). The second commandment, "Love your neighbor as yourself," follows the first: "Love the Lord your God with all your heart and with all your soul and with all your mind" (Matt. 22:37). Our love for God leads us to accept and love our neighbor.

Today's psychology of selfism is light years away from what Jesus and John are talking about. Instead of providing the healthy state of thinking of ourselves no more highly than we should, as we look not only to our own interests but to the interests of others, selfism only increases our drive for being self-fulfilled. We are driven by sensuality, competition, the need to get more and more as we restrain ourselves less and less. John White believes the selfism trend has taken only one decade to achieve alarming momentum. He writes:

> Far from being an aid to loving my neighbor, self-love is that which leads in the end to riding rough-shod over him, trampling him to death if need be . . . . Self-love in this sense is self-lust—the lust of the flesh, the lust of the eye and the pride of life, none of which are of the Father but of this world and are symptomatic of the hedonistic age in which we live. It is worldly, thoroughly worldly, in the most biblical sense of the term.[8]

Shades of 1 John 2:16! Where will selfism take us? John makes our choice clear: "The world and its desires pass away, but the man who does the will of God lives forever" (1 John 2:17).

John's words echo down the tunnels of time and bring their warning to sophisticated, high-tech believers who plan to ride space shuttles into the twenty-first century:

> Little children, guard yourselves from the unreal,
> the counterfeit, from anything that takes the place
> due God alone. Above all, guard yourselves from the
> *self!*

## *Test Your Faith*

Do you know for a fact that God truly loves you and you have eternal life? Get a better understanding of this truth by answering the following questions:

1. My prayer life is:
   a. Exciting
   b. Neglected
   c. Plodding along
   d. Up and down.

List some reasons for your answer.

2. In this chapter, William Barclay is quoted: "We are apt to think that prayer is asking God for what we want, whereas true prayer is asking God for what He wants." Do you agree or disagree. Why?

3. In your opinion, is praying, "If it be your will, Lord," a cop-out or a proper precaution? Explain your answer.

4. Saint Augustine is supposed to have prayed: "Oh, God, make me more pure, but not right away." Do you identify? In what way?

5. What is "the sin unto death"?
   a. Unforgivable sins like murder
   b. Apostasy

c. Backsliding
d. Blasphemy against the Holy Spirit.

6. In 1 John 5:18, the apostle writes: "We know that anyone born of God does not continue to sin." How does this verse make you feel?
a. Encouraged
b. Defeated
c. Nervous
d. Puzzled.
In what areas of life do you seem to continue to sin? How do you cope? (See the rest of v. 18, also vv. 19, 20.)

7. In your opinion, what is the worst kind of idolatry?
a. Materialism
b. Selfism
c. Hedonism
d. Humanism.
Explain your answer.

---

## Notes

1. 1 John 5:13.
2. Bruce Larson, *Believe and Belong* (Old Tappan, NJ: Fleming H. Revell, Co., 1982), p. 15.
3. W. E. Vine, *Vine's Expository Dictionary of Old and New Testament Words* (Old Tappan, NJ: Fleming H. Revell Co., 1981), p. 298.
4. Curtis Vaughn, *1,2,3 John* (Grand Rapids: Zondervan Publishing House, 1970), pp. 128, 129.
5. Adapted from Lloyd Ogilvie, *Praying With Power* (Ventura, CA: Regal Books, 1983), p. 106.
6. William Barclay, *The Letters of John and Jude* Daily Study Bible (Edinburgh: The St. Andrew Press, 1958), p. 137.
7. See "An Unknown Christian," *The Kneeling Christian* (Grand Rapids: Zondervan Publishing House, 1971), p. 110.
8. Ibid., pp. 110, 111.
9. W. L. Vaswig, "For My Part," *Response, the Newsletter of Preaching and Prayer Ministries*, vol. 9, no. 3, Summer 1984, p. 2.
10. Vaughn, *1,2,3 John* p. 132.
11. Ibid., p. 133.

12. John Stott, *The Epistles of John* (Grand Rapids: Wm. B. Eerdmans Publishing Co., 1970), p. 193.

13. Ibid., p. 194.

14. Robert Raines, *To Kiss the Joy* (Waco, TX: Word, Inc., 1973), pp. 27, 28. Raines quotes from Gay Talese, "The Kingdom and the Power" *New York Times*, (New York: World Publishing Co., 1969), p. 13.

15. Vine, *Expository Dictionary*, p. 298.

16. Paul C. Vitz, *Psychology As Religion* (Grand Rapids: Wm. B. Eerdmans Publishing Co., 1977), chaps. 6 and 8.

17. John White, *Flirting with the World* (Wheaton: Harold Shaw Publishers, 1982), pp. 120, 121.

18. Ibid., pp. 123, 124.

# Epilogue
# The Final Inch

In *The First Circle,* one of his novels about life in Russian prison camps, Alexander Solzhenitsyn lets us eavesdrop on a conversation between two prisoners. Sologdin, middle-aged, bearded and wise, has spent years in confinement. Nerzhin, a brilliant young mathematician, has been imprisoned a shorter time. As they cut wood together in the biting cold, Sologdin offers to share "certain of his rules" with the younger man to help him deal with the long years of imprisonment ahead.

Nerzhin eagerly agrees and Sologdin lays down his first rule, which deals with how to face difficulties and handle failure:

> Failures must be considered the cue for further application of effort and concentration of will power ... Overcoming the increased difficulties is all the more valuable because in failure the growth of the person performing the task takes place in proportion to the difficulty encountered!

Sologdin's ideal aim is not success, power, prestige or status. When you are in prison, these goals become far too common. For Sologdin, the ultimate goal is always *growth— developing into a mature, complete person.*

He continues by referring to his "Rule of the Final Inch,"

which must always be followed when trying to complete a quality piece of work. Sologdin warns Nerzhin against those moments of fatigue or self-satisfaction when he might be tempted to settle for second-best while the work is still "not quite right." The rule of the Final Inch precludes shirking the task, putting if off or minding how long it takes. He who seeks to cover the Final Inch knows that "one's purpose lies not in completing things faster, but in the attainment of perfection."[1]

It's my guess the apostle John and Sologdin would have had some good chats together had they both served time in the same prison. John knew that the realm of the Final Inch is where all Christians dwell. In the beginning, the Final Inch seems to be a short, easy step. Sooner or later (for most of us, sooner), we learn it is actually one long journey in the same direction. Christians are the "not-yet-ones," always pressing onward, not quite finished, but looking forward to a state of glory that is beyond imagining. As John put it: "Now we are children of God, and what we will be has not yet been made known. But we know that when he appears, we shall be like him, for we shall see him as he is" (1 John 3:2).

Paul also understood the Final Inch: "Not that I have already obtained all this, or have already been made perfect . . . But one thing I do: Forgetting what is behind and straining toward what is ahead, I press on toward the goal to win the prize for which God has called me heavenward in Christ Jesus" (Phil. 3:12-14).

We began our study of John's letter wanting to know how to be Christians without being perfect. As we close the book, we see that he was really writing about how to be a Christian while being perfected or, if you prefer, how to be a Christian while in God's process.

Truly, we are in God's process and His goal for us is that we be perfect—whole, complete, mature—*grown up!* And what of our failures? Like Sologdin, we welcome them as a way to grow. For the not-yet-ones, failure always leads toward eventual success. We have already overcome the world by placing our faith in Christ. We continue to overcome as we obey, love and believe. We trust Christ and love one another. If only these be done, we will cover the Final Inch with room enough to spare.

## Notes

1. Alexander Solzhenitsyn, *The First Circle,* trans. Thomas P. Whitney (New York: Harper & Row Pubs., Inc. 1968), p. 139.